CORNED
BEEF,
KNISHES,
AND
CHRIST

CORNED BEEF, KNISHES, AND CHRIST

The Story of a
20th-century Levite

ZOLA LEVITT

TYNDALE HOUSE PUBLISHERS, INC.
Wheaton, Illinois

COVERDALE HOUSE PUBLISHERS LTD.
London, England

Library of Congress Catalog Card Number 74-19647
ISBN 8423-0440-1
Copyright © 1975 by Tyndale House Publishers, Inc.,
Wheaton, Illinois 60187. All rights reserved.
First printing, January 1975
Printed in the United States of America

To Yvonne
Now, as then,
the most beautiful girl in the world!

CONTENTS

1
The Night I Saw Jesus

Jesus is a much taller man than I would have imagined. When I saw him, he was wearing a maroon-colored robe, very ceremonious, hanging in folds like fine drapes. It stood open about six inches down the center, showing an off-white tunic underneath.

I was slumped down in an armchair where I had been reading and meditating. He was standing directly in front of me, and I had to crook my neck to look at his face. I remember thinking that he must have been very tall—6'4'' perhaps—because it was hard to look up so high. Alternately, I remember thinking that I must be seeing something unreal because the figure seemed entirely *too* tall for a man.

I was unable to make out his facial features at all. Either they "disappeared into the ceiling" or I was too shocked to see details. I did seem to be able to see his hair, which was light brown and gently waved down to his shoulders, rather like the great paintings of the Lord.

But I seemed somehow to perceive his expression nevertheless: it was benevolent and good-humored. If he had spoken, he might have said, "Relax, I'm here, child."

But he didn't speak, and he didn't have to. I got the message.

Then, just at the instant I began to realize that I was looking Jesus Christ in the face, he disappeared. Vanished.

And I panicked because I went blind! I remember being relieved that the seeming apparition had disappeared, but I was looking into solid gray murk before my eyes. I couldn't focus on anything. It was like looking into clouds out of a plane. There was just nothing to be seen. I turned my head and looked at another angle but I still couldn't see.

Then everything came back with a pop. There was a sound, and my familiar bedroom came back to me.

My heart wasn't pounding and I didn't really feel too out of sorts, despite the eerie happening. I just sat there realizing I'd seen God. I was a little afraid to move.

I got my thoughts back together after a minute or so and I sort of tried to evaluate the event. "After all," I thought, "I've been sitting here reading a long time. I'm tired. Maybe I just drifted off to sleep for a moment. Maybe it was a dream. Maybe I just psyched myself up with my Bible reading and thinking about Christ. Maybe it was a kind of wishful daydream."

I had been deeply considering turning my life over to Christ. People had been witnessing to me, making me "see" the Lord. Perhaps in my skepticism I had conjured him up in order to evaluate him firsthand.

But I didn't really believe all that. I thought I'd really seen Christ. You can evaluate it as you like, but to me it was very real.

I can't remember if it was that same night that I finally went to Christ in prayer. I spent many nights in my bedroom armchair, reading the Bible and thinking about God and my life. You may think it was extraordinary that I could actually see Christ and still resist giving my life over to him, but that's the stubbornness of my Jewish character. Thousands of my brothers in Israel resisted him every day when he was there. (And thousands received him, too, it should be remembered.) In more belligerent moments I used to tell smug Gentiles, "If it weren't for the courageous Jews who walked with Christ and formed your first churches, you wouldn't have any Christianity." (Probably they would have, by some other of God's means. But my patience with Christians who curse the Jews is awfully thin.)

It was tough for me to come to Christ, and not because I was Jewish. It was mostly because I believed that I knew better how to run my affairs than he did. I fall back into that belief every other day, as things are now, even though I know it's ridiculous. For me, giving up on Zola Levitt and letting Jesus take over is the hard part. I gather we all have some trouble there.

The manner in which I finally "joined the flock" is a long story and I'll save it for later. I think it would serve better if I say something about the "old man," the one who died when Christ took over with his gift of rebirth, before getting to my big moment.

That "old man" is dead but he rolls in his grave. I often want to tell him to "Rest in Peace," because he never had any.

2
"Max, Do You Call This Lox?"

I was raised to believe that the Jews were the best people, and in the heart of me I still do.

I was raised in a Jewish neighborhood and my father had a Jewish store. My mother shopped, painstakingly, in a succession of those Jewish markets where each shop specializes in its own field—one for fish, one for poultry, one for beef, one for baked goods, one for dairy foods, etc., etc.

Today's supermarkets are much more convenient. But something has been lost.

My father bought my clothes in Pittsburgh's wholesale garment district—this store for shirts, that one for pants, a third one for ties, etc., etc. Today's department stores are much more convenient, but again, something has been lost.

Let me take you on a couple of shopping trips. You'll get to meet my parents....

I can remember going out with Mama every day for food when I was a preschooler. Food was bought daily because it had to be absolutely fresh in keeping with the kosher laws. Some staples could be kept in their appropriate places in our divided kitchen, but the ice box was not trusted to keep meats and dairy foods uncontaminated. The divided kitchen, of course, had to do with the complete segregation of meat foods and their derivatives, from milk foods and their derivatives. Also, Passover dishes, milk and meat, were kept separate from year-round dishes, in closed cupboards. So my mother maintained four sets of dishes and silverware, like any good kosher housewife.

We would wait until the ice man came in the morning to put a nice fresh block of ice in our old wooden refrigerator and then we would head out to shop. I considered the trips to the various stores, greeting so many different people, a lot of fun. So did Mama.

We would head up Mellon Street for the bakery, fruits and vegetables, and fish, and come back down St. Clair Street for the meat. The meat was picked up last and rushed to the ice box quickly.

Part of the fun at the stores was staying friendly with the merchant without getting hoodwinked at the counter. The baker would have loved to sell his day-old stuff to my mama but she was too sharp for that. At the fish store we would be greeted by the proprietor in the doorway, dangling in Mama's face a smoked fish of which he was especially proud.

You see, nowadays the fellow behind the counter at the food store doesn't know food. Who smokes his own fish nowadays? And how often, when you go into a modern bakery, can you interview the baker? Who makes his own cream cheese

6

today, or pickles his own pickles? Who can you complain to when the stuff isn't quite right?

To whom can you say, "Max, do you call this lox? Do you feed it to your own kids?"

And conversely, nowadays who argues with you when you return something to the food store? The guy at the A & P gives you a refund cheerfully, having no real idea of what you find lacking. But Max used to say, "Lox, yes, I call it lox and to mine own kids I feed it. If you don't know real lox don't into my store come complaining!"

We're not used to personal attention these days. If my mother went into the produce store for some tomatoes the boss's son or daughter would come out from behind the counter and whisper, "Mrs. Levitt, tomatoes we got, and plenty, but today take celery too! What celery we got today! Celery like this we haven't had for you for a long time...."

I don't mean to stereotype Jews, because there are more kinds of Jews around than of any other people. When your ancestors have lived all over the world for 2,000 years, "variety you got." These are just my recollections of the characters in my neighborhood, roughly during the period of the second World War. The peculiar speech constructions, the sonorous music of which is impossible to convey in writing, come from the Yiddish tongue, one of the world's richest languages.

At the meat store my mother wouldn't buy the meats in the showcase. She didn't know how long they'd been on display and she didn't trust the butcher to tell her the straight story. When she bought, the butcher had to have his son take over the counter while he went into the big "cold room" to cut our meat fresh off the hanging sides.

Shopping was a matter of hours and made eating all the more fun. I miss it.

Certain food shopping was the prerogative of the man of the house only. Buying corned beef, for example, was a matter of shrewd judgment not trusted to women in my family. I waited eagerly for Sunday when my father had time to go up Mellon Street to the wonderful store that pickled its own beef, and personally negotiate the purchase.

My father was an expert on corned beef and on negotiating.

We would saunter into the little store as though we weren't interested in buying anything at all. We would casually, and with a disapproving air, glance over the meats in the showcase, and then appear to be leaving. The manager would take his cue and approach us as we neared the door.

"Mr. Levitt, my friend," he would gush. "And little what's-his-name here. How are you, how are you? How may I serve you?"

His act of receiving royalty didn't even fool me, let alone my canny old man, but it was all part of the routine.

Father would say, "Well, Sol, we was interested maybe in a little corned beef for Sunday, but ..." and he would shrug toward the showcase as if Sol should realize that his meats were far beneath us.

Sol would smile broadly and whisper to my father. The whisper technique was a staple of the local salesmanship. "Joe," he would hiss. "For you, from the cellar!" This meant that the boss would go downstairs and select absolutely fresh meat from the pickling brine for good customers like us.

My father would express an elaborately nonchalant interest in sampling the good stuff from the cellar and Sol would hustle off. I sometimes fleetingly wondered if the good stuff was in the showcase and the bad stuff in the cellar, and my father was being duped, but nothing would be transacted until my father could taste the actual meat.

Sol would reappear at the head of the cellar stairs dangling a piece of corned beef in his hand and my father would take it from him and taste it, with a faraway look. Sol and I would stand breathless, awaiting the verdict.

Occasionally other, less expert customers would watch for my father's reaction, trusting his air of the distinguished gourmet.

At length Father would say, in Yiddish, "For the goyim." In other words, the stuff was only good enough for gentiles to eat. This meant no disrespect for the gentiles, but was an idiom to grade the meat. If it were really bad my father might walk out without a word. If it were exceptionally good he would buy some with a rather reluctant attitude. After all, you couldn't let the pickler get a swelled head; there was always next Sunday to think about.

Part of this negotiating was aimed at affecting the price. If my father could convince Sol that the meat was really not up to snuff, the price might inch down.

In the synagogue my father and Sol were true brothers, of course. Spiritually they loved one another and felt a great kinship. But corned beef was a serious matter, and a place of business was no scene of sentiment.

Buying clothes was the same story. My father and I would go down to the garment district and act as if we were just passing through. We'd go into a store and be waited on by the boss. (My father dealt only with the boss, and in his own store, a five-and-ten, he would personally wait on his Jewish customers.)

Father would say, "Hello, Sid. Maybe you have something in a suit for the boy?"

Whatever Sid would come up with would be barely adequate, of course, and price would be a matter of the relative skill of the bargainers. My father was able to buy me name-brand clothing at a third of the retail price.

My father was on the receiving end of such bargaining in his own establishment, of course. The merchandise had fixed prices, but the salesmen who came around from the wholesale houses would haggle. My father did all of his own buying, going into the largest warehouses in Pittsburgh and personally selecting his dozen of this and dozen of that.

I remember a scene in the showroom of a large company where my father picked out glassware. The company was set up to deliver train-carloads to big department stores nationally, but my father insisted upon inspecting the stuff and picking out his own small order in the showroom. He was in the company of professional buyers ordering many thousands of units but he considered himself as important as Kresge. ("He came over on the boat with me," he revealed one day about his illustrious competitor.)

The salesman was mocking my father behind his back on that day I remember. As father would look at each single glass and dish the salesman would say, "How about a hundred gross of those, Mr. Levitt?" and he would grin at his colleagues across the store. My father would order his dozen without seeming to notice that he was the butt of sneers.

When he had completed his order he would go to the front counter and ask for the same discount that the big buyers got. That was preposterous but the salesman thought he was such a silly character that he usually gave him the cut rate. Kresge's probably never figured out how little Joe Levitt was able to meet their prices.

On the way out of the showroom that day I said, "Do you know they're laughing at you in there?"

"Yep," he replied, pocketing his receipt with the big discount.

He rarely had anything shipped. He normally drove his car to the loading gate and took his small order home in the trunk. I got to be a more and more valuable member of the family enterprise as I grew bigger and could load heavier boxes.

At the loading gate, where trucks were lined up to receive huge shipments, my father would open each box to be sure there were no broken glasses. This exasperated the shippers no end but sure enough, my father would find a broken glass from time to time. He would present it to the foreman and receive a new one, and until he was satisfied, Macy's and Gimbels could wait in the driveways.

As a teen-ager I was concerned with the appearance of things and I thought he looked foolish. But one day while I was standing in a showroom watching him do his thing, an owner of the company spoke to me. He had been watching me and he said simply, "We value your father's business."

Modern times caught up with my father and passed him by. His little store was in the way of Urban Renewal when it came to Pittsburgh and my father, past sixty years old, had to make a fresh start in a new location. He worked hard, fighting a Sears & Roebuck in the next block, and he hung on for some five years.

Retirement was out of the question for him, and his doctors only warned him to take it very easy. He was to remain seated most of the day, take naps, and never overstrain. He had a dreadful heart condition and was weakened by a colostomy. But he opened his little store every day, the same as Mr. Sears and Mr. Roebuck, and his customers remained faithful.

One day there was a terrible snowstorm and my father couldn't get his car out of the driveway. He walked the two miles or so to the store and opened it only slightly behind schedule. He was hospitalized and died shortly after.

My mother is still alive, and still in Pittsburgh, in one of the few remaining neighborhoods where one can buy fish from a fish man and chicken from a chicken man.

I've gotten ahead of myself in introducing my parents. I should mention that being raised Jewish was more than just living in a Jewish neighborhood or eating kosher food. I went to Hebrew School and Sunday school for many years, was Bar Mitzvah and confirmed. In a later chapter I will be recounting my early "Jewishness," but suffice it to say that I was very Jewish indeed, and still am. They didn't teach that the Messiah—Jesus—had already come in my parochial education, but they made me know what being Jewish was!

I know my teachers had the best of intentions. They simply didn't know the truth, or that the truth would set them free. They were highly devout, respectable men, versed in Scripture and reverent toward God. In God's eyes they must have been the best of all possible unbelievers.

I would go to Hebrew School every day right after public school and stay about two hours. Hebrew School didn't meet on Fridays because of the Sabbath. We students were a difficult bunch, having sat all day in regular school before arriving, full of mischief, at the little building adjoining the synagogue.

The lessons went slowly and we were always up to pranks and tricks. I know my teachers believed in God; if they hadn't had some kind of spiritual strength to restrain themselves they would have killed us.

Hebrew School was devoted entirely to the language, and its application in reading The Talmud (The Law). In Sunday school we took up the Scriptures, and current Judaism. There I learned the timeless stories of Abraham, Isaac, and Jacob, and the beautiful Psalms, which we memorized

We also breathlessly followed the progress of Israel, which became an independent Jewish state when I was about nine years old. We understood that the land returned to our people had suffered much in our absence. Trees were needed, and water to irrigate the fields. And many pioneers who would be willing to restore the promised land to its former fertility and beauty. Many have laid claim to the land given Abraham by God, but none have loved it and cared for it like the Jews.

Our Sunday school teacher put up a poster of a tree with blank outlines of leaves on its branches. Each child was to bring a dime to class each Sunday and the teacher would paste a leaf in a blank. Soon the tree would be filled, our money would be sent to our brothers in Israel, and a tree would be actually planted in our names.

During my school years, I brought enough dimes for a whole tree and one of those trees over there is mine.

When I went to high school I was mainly interested in music and girls; there is no "Jewish life" that corresponds to what is called a "Christian life." We Jews did tend to congregate together, dating within our own group and skipping school days on our holidays, but as I was not Orthodox there was no special "behavior," no rites to be done as part of daily living. Prayer was done in groups at the synagogue on Sabbath, and otherwise one merely was Jewish by being with Jewish people. (I should say that there were "better Jews" than I, who regularly attended synagogue and wrapped their arms every morning with the Tifilin, and thus encountered God on a daily basis.)

As for the Christians, I didn't know who they were—that is, I couldn't tell a Christian from a gentile. I was taught that people are divided into two categories, Jews and others, and this is borne out in the Old Testament. My father regarded church-going people not as seriously religious, but as merely carrying on an ineffective copy of Jewish worship. In some cases I think he was right.

"Jesus Christ" was a cuss word to us Jews, and we of course had no realization of the fullness of Christianity. This is still true of the Jews, by and large, and it's because nobody has told them anything.

I paid little attention to my high school courses. I had the idea, all the way through high school and ten years of college that the studies were pointless and silly. And by golly, I was right. What there is of this life that is vitally important—the fact that God is alive and working with his children—was not indicated to me in secular or religious studies. My grades came out so-so and I had to take an intelligence test to get into college.

I didn't know why I was going to college, other than that it was a must for Jewish kids. I had no idea of what I wanted to study. My father wanted me to take over the family store, of course, but I had no real interest in business. My lack of scholastic abilities seemed to rule out any serious professional studies, like medicine or law, both quite acceptable in the Jewish community. And my real inner desire was to study music, not because I had any particular zeal for it but because it was fun.

I registered at the University of Pittsburgh in Liberal Arts. I didn't know then what "Liberal Arts" were, and I don't now, but it seemed a way to delay choosing what I wanted to be when I grew up. I took a smattering of courses in various fields, mainly deciding which ones by how late they started in the mornings.

If this sounds like I was a smart-alecky, spoiled Jewish kid, it's because I was.

3
"What Is Sociology?"

College was largely a nonstop party for me. I joined a fraternity, Jewish of course, learned to drink large amounts of beer while appearing to enjoy it, and continued to explore the world of women.

Occasionally I studied, on the nights before exams, and I barely kept my head above water academically. I was a little unnerved, personally, about what I was doing and where it might lead me, but I had no conception of self-discipline or how to lead an orderly life.

I think I was an average college student.

The best part of college was my work as the entertainment director of my fraternity. While I was next to failing out of school, I was probably the best entertainment director a fraternity could ever ask for.

Instead of just hiring some kind of entertainment for our fraternity affairs I wrote an original musical play for each social event. Since they came biweekly I probably did ten times more play-writing than studying at Pitt. I wish I had those playscripts and musical scores today; I learned more from that work than I ever did in the classroom.

Would that kind of thing be in the province of God? Our Father, who said, "I will use the wrath of men to praise me"—might he have thought, "I'll train this fellow as a writer and musician, and then when he comes to me I'll put his experience to good use"?

In any case, the fun I was having staging my little plays certainly beat the tedium of my academic courses. I don't mean to sound ungrateful or unappreciative of man's knowledge, but those courses seemed very phony. I remember the first day in sociology; the professor fixed a solemn stare on our class and intoned, "What is sociology?" We spent the rest of the term on that question, as far as I could tell, and never answered it.

I took some math, some history, some psychology, and a music appreciation course which I really enjoyed. My only high grades came in the music studies and I was finally able to convince my parents that I belonged in music school.

My music professor managed to get me a small scholarship at his alma mater, Miami of Ohio, and I went off after a year at Pitt. My parents were a bit skeptical ("What kind of business is that for a Jew?") but they realized, as I did, that I might fail out if I tried anything else.

I signed up in music education, aiming to get a teaching certificate and support myself some great day. My parents were still providing the money for my education but I wanted to be independent of that.

At Miami I loved the coursework in music but

the education courses were idiotic. I know whereof I speak about education; I was eventually to get my certificate and teach, but to find it impossible to survive against boards of education and ludicrous school rules.

I became really interested in educational methods but it seemed to me that no creative thinking was welcome in that field. I stayed at Miami two years, after which the faculty told me I "was not teacher material." "Teacher material" is made out of people who can take orders, worship the latest theories and regard children as experimental animals, I think. In that I had many original ideas and was a good musician I looked out of place in the music education department.

There were some good things at Miami —extracurricular, as usual. There I met the sweet girl who was to become my first wife.

Gay was so pretty and so kind to everyone that I felt almost guilty marrying her. She was a Catholic who did not practice her faith, and she fit as well as anybody with a Jew who did not practice his. She sympathized with my problems with the education department and was willing to marry me despite my not being "teacher material." It was the best kind of young love, suitable for kids.

Since I was not going to graduate at Miami without mending my ways and becoming what they thought of as teacher material, I undertook to transfer colleges again. I did it the same way; I went to my favorite professor, asked him where he graduated and got him to phone them and get me in.

And so I ended up at Ithaca College.

My young wife and I—she was nineteen and I was twenty-one—took a small apartment in Ithaca, N.Y., and I transferred my credits and resumed my music education courses.

The most difficulty I had in these transfers of colleges was repeating the courses in which I hadn't done well. And the one that haunted me most was English composition. I always got bad grades in creative writing because I did things differently than my classmates. I was not "writer material," I suppose.

I had thought that Ithaca would be a more modern and intellectually stimulating place to study than my foregoing colleges, judging by the personality of the professor who sent me there, but again I had my troubles. The future teachers were judged by two old biddies who hadn't been in a classroom for a century between them, and again I didn't look like teacher material. (They even used the same expression!)

Too, I was becoming a pretty good musician by this time and the characteristic of music teachers was supposed to be that they were so passionately interested in educational theory that they didn't have time to be good players. Actually the old maxim, "Those who can't do, teach," explained the situation better. The education students were normally just untalented practitioners.

In the midst of all that struggle we learned that a baby was on the way. I began to wonder if I was "father material."

By the time Mark was born, at the end of that school year, I was preparing to transfer again, having been pronounced unfit by Ithaca College as teacher material.

Now you may wonder if it didn't occur to me that all those experts might have been right. Maybe I really *wasn't* teacher material. Maybe you're thinking, "He was just stuck on himself and he couldn't get along with anybody."

Well, there's truth in that, but I *was* teacher material. When I did finally get out and teach I had a wonderful time and so did the children. It's been said of me that I was not teacher material, writer material, musician material or even Christian material. But somehow, in the plan of God, I go on teaching, writing, playing, and worshiping with great satisfaction, and I only wait to meet my Lord who loves me like crazy.

I took my wife and my new little boy back home to Pittsburgh, and I entered Duquesne University, determined to graduate if it killed me. I just had to support my family, so I went into a one-and-a-half-year teacher-material act. I spoke to no one, but smiled all the time. I learned to use the dumb expressions of education-ese and concealed my interest in music. I dressed like everyone else and I kept all my thoughts to myself, never expressing an idea that had not been said first by someone else.

In that manner I got my degree and my teaching certificate.

I got a job at the Pittsburgh schools teaching music to elementary schoolers, and as I suspected, they could learn much more and much faster than my professors had supposed. I was in a slum neighborhood but I had my fifth graders able to compose their own songs, and my little first graders able to dance in correct rhythms to various time signatures.

But I got caught.

These creepy people from the Board of Education would storm my classroom without warning, supposedly to be of help, and they would be horrified at the goings-on. One time I was caught playing a Mozart sonata on the piano with my shoes off. Another time my sixth graders and I were in the middle of a tremendous laugh about something and the sober-and-sad Board supervisor came in.

The time I remember best was when I had some college music theory on the blackboard and was getting my fifth graders to understand it. I had the circle of fifths, a graph of the various key signatures, drawn on the board, and the kids were busily working out the names of the sharps and flats so that they could extend their own compositions into all keys. Some of them had already produced excellent songs, correctly written in difficult key signatures, and I was very proud of them.

Enter the supervisor from the Board.

He came in like an executioner, with a loathsome smile that indicated he didn't like me any more than I liked him. The kids weren't fooled. Children are terrifically sensitive to atmospheres, especially the slum-neighborhood kids, whom the Board thought of as stupid. Those kids who have to live by their wits are always smarter than the sheltered ones, I've found. But they aren't good "student material."

The supervisor wanted to know, in whispers to me, why we weren't working on the material for that day as given in the Board syllabus. The children were supposed to be learning to sing "When Johnny Comes Marching Home" by rote that day. Mine were able to *compose* better stuff than that, but they were supposed to be stupid.

The supervisor asked me what the material on the blackboard was, and I suddenly realized that this supervisor of public school music in a large modern city did not even understand the circle of fifths. It would be like a surgeon walking in and asking what an aspirin was.

You'll forgive me, I hope, when I tell you I quit at the end of the year. The children threw a going-away party for me such as that "disadvantaged" school had never seen. It seemed that every mother in the neighborhood had baked something for the kids to bring to my classroom and we partied all day.

I sent cake and cookies around to the other teachers all day because I had enough to start a small bakery. But after school I went around to say good-bye to everybody and I saw the goodies in the wastebaskets. When I went down to the office to say good-bye to the principal I saw his cake in the wastebasket and I asked about that.

"You didn't eat that stuff, did you?" he exclaimed. And he explained to me that the kitchens in the neighborhood were filthy. No prejudice, mind you, he huffed, but they grew up on filthy food, and we up-towners would probably get very sick if we ate it.

I couldn't help it. I ate a big piece of it right in front of him while I said good-bye.

And I didn't get sick. Love agrees with me.

I registered at Indiana University for a master's

degree that fall and my wife and I amassed all the money we could in the summer. My thinking was that I couldn't bear teaching any longer. The only thing I got any kick out of was music and I was going to study a straight applied music course and perfect my oboe playing. I could safely say that I detested schools, boards of education, and everything connected with being teacher material.

I loved children and I loved music, so I decided to have my own and play my own.

4
Blind Alleys

The master's degree was a lot of hard work and I lost some of my wise-guy attitude toward the world. I had to really dig in and practice my instrument and study my books.

But it was a kind of cop-out too. I knew in my heart that I just didn't have a better idea than going back to school, and in truth, I still didn't know what I wanted to be when I grew up. Here I was, a husband and father, undertaking more schooling just to escape the realities of earning a living. I had my legitimate beefs against the school teaching world, but I felt very guilty when a friend said, "Why don't you stay in and fight it if it needs changing?"

I did very well on the master's, as it happened, getting the degree in one year and graduating with high honors. But it was a miserable year on the home front. My young wife had worked full-time and my son Mark spent his first year in the world with baby-sitters most of the time.

I was grateful to Gay for putting me through that year and I told her so, but I was overwhelmed secretly by my own selfishness.

I applied for some jobs in college music teaching but the market was requiring a doctorate, or at least studies past the master's degree. So I enrolled again. I started my doctorate in music.

It wasn't going to be hard on the family that year because I won a teaching assistantship at the university and Gay and Mark could stay at home all day. I realized that I had only the vaguest interest in becoming "Dr. Levitt," but again, I didn't know what else to do.

And I knew my marriage was breaking up, and I didn't care. Gay and I had become "just friends" at best, conversing politely when necessary and basically living two different lives. It wasn't that we fought; we had just grown so far apart that it wasn't worth a good fight. We married far too young, at a time when it seemed we were "made for each other," and we had become strangers as we grew in the same household.

If we'd had the slightest knowledge of God or how he sanctified the marriage vows, that situation would not have happened. But we lived in a secular, intellectual environment where the real values of love and faith take a back seat to the worldly values of education and cash.

During that year we separated and finally divorced.

I had intended to have another go at it with her at some future time, but she remarried three months after the divorce. I was suddenly alone in the world. And I didn't care about that either.

Also during that year I finally "made the grade" in professional music. I won an audition to perform with the New Orleans Philharmonic. My oboe playing, rather quickly gotten together in graduate school, was good enough to get me a job I considered really interesting. I was to report in the fall following that first year of my doctorate.

I spent that summer working in a women's shoe store. Any man interested in how women think should sell them shoes. It was a learning experience, to say the least.

I spent the following year in the New Orleans Philharmonic and the one after that in the San Antonio Symphony. I also did some conducting, as I had done earlier with the Pittsburgh Savoyards Opera Company, in various theatres in San Antonio. I had several successful years making music, but I wasn't happy. My much-revered professional music world turned out to be a disappointment.

The musicians were not "artists." They were a bunch of normal people who happened to play music for a living. The conductors were intolerable. I played under men of fame and fortune on the podium who could barely read music, and whose maniacal domination of their orchestras made one think of Hitler.

The opera, where I was a conductor for a while, was a madhouse of talented people frantically gouging one another out of roles. Their intrigues and rumors rivaled those on the stage. People adopted phony accents to appear cultured. Conductors would lose their places in the score at rehearsal, stop the orchestra on some pretense, and then start back at the beginning for another try at following the music.

I'm not talking about amateurs. This is the professional level, where folks are exhorted to pay cash to symphony foundations and then appear at concerts in their formal dress.

I never could get the hang of bootlicking the rich so that the orchestra could get contributions. We actually had a case where some rich woman brought her monotone daughter down to the rehearsal hall for an audition with our musical director. I was to play the piano. We hoked up the whole thing, told the old lady her gal had a great voice, accepted her check, and went home.

Another time, when I was being groomed as a conductor, I was introduced to some fat-cat patrons as "Dr. Levitt." I pointed out right there that I did not as yet hold the doctorate. I was told afterward to keep my mouth shut during such introductions.

I don't mean to say it was all phony. A lot of people give their hearts and souls to music and they mean it. But almost anything else sullied by ego trips and profit motives, music is "vanity, vanity." I met some competent and sincere instrumentalists and conductors along the way, but they were invariably depressed by what went on around them.

I was more satisfied with music when I stopped doing it for my full-time livelihood. I began just to do fill-in work for players who were ill, or when an orchestra needed extra players for a big work. I toured the symphony orchestras of Milwaukee, Indianapolis, Austin, Fort Worth—nothing really "big time," but very pleasant since I just had to play, not attend the parties.

Most enjoyable in my musical career were Glen Campbell Show tours. I was a "pick-up" musician who joined the tours as they passed through my area. When Glen sang, 20,000 people came out and we sure didn't have to raise any funds. And unlike the "maestros" of the concert podium, Campbell turned out to be a genuine, nice guy.

I have to tell a story in passing that I can never forget. Everywhere we appeared with Glen Campbell, the girls came out in force, squealing and swooning in the grand tradition. But at one stop I noticed a lady about forty just hanging on the backstage barrier and calling out for the star.

I went over to her and said, "Ma'am, Mr. Campbell has left already. He can't afford to get caught in these crowds."

"Oh, dear, oh, dear," she fretted, and she looked next to tears.

I asked, "Why are you so upset?"

She said, "This is my wedding anniversary and my husband is at home waiting for me. But I'll tell you something—if Glen would just take me away with him I'd never go home again!"

That's show biz.

I just couldn't stay with it. I let my union card expire and quit playing music.

My second "career" came out of my desperation to be happy in this life. I went to see a psychoanalyst. At the time, I was at the peak of my musical activities, performing with a major symphony orchestra, acting as assistant conductor with a fine opera company, and directing soldier shows at a large Army base on the side. I was making the equivalent of three full-time incomes, had girl friends galore, was called by name in every fancy restaurant in town, and was next to killing myself in my unhappiness.

Somehow I had no peace. I couldn't get to sleep at night. I was only twenty-five and I thought there was real danger of my harming myself.

The analyst was a terrifically brilliant guy who was a fake in terms of degrees (which he didn't have) but a genius in terms of help. He continually quoted Jesus as a well-adjusted character, and I found out that he'd gone to seminary in his youth. By the way he conducted his life I didn't think he was a Christian but I'm not the judge of that. Homer was pure kindness and pure forgiveness, and he taught high self-esteem as a way of life. "To him that hath it shall be given," he would intone, certifying Jesus as a truly self-loving personality. He said that Jesus' power came from his superlative self-confidence, that we must love ourselves first in order to be able to give love elsewhere.

I remember comparing this philosophy with a statement by Eric Hoffer: "The trouble is we really do love our neighbor as ourselves; when we hate ourselves we hate our neighbors."

I don't mean to bring up matters of gravity here, but rather to stress the fact that even the so-called scientific process of psychoanalysis borrows heavily from the Gospels. Homer, in carrying out the Christian philosophy he had absorbed as a youth, was the first example of forgiveness I'd run into on earth. The God my mother trained me to pray to was the real Father in Heaven, but he was made to be a very remote God. I might offer praise and pleas, but I wasn't necessarily to expect an answer. But Jesus responds, as Homer did.

The change Homer wrought in me had to do with my forgiving myself for my sins and taking a more forgiving view toward the sins of my neighbors. It did me a world of good, but Jesus is more to the point. Forgiving ourselves is an arduous task; apparently God felt that we needed forgiveness from outside ourselves when he sent his Son.

It's hard to simplify a psychoanalytic process that went on for almost three years on a nearly daily basis. Suffice it to say that it was my first course in human relations and it served me well.

Homer had told me that people would sense my new "mental health" and that I should feel free to counsel them. And sure enough, I began to be a sounding board for my colleagues in the orchestra and the soldiers at the base. People wanted to tell me their troubles. Eventually Homer came to think it would be a good idea if he trained me as an analyst in his clinic. I was like an intern. He let me use an office, and when he had calls from clients who couldn't pay the standard fees he would refer them to me. I started out charging three dollars per hour for my newfound "wisdom."

It may be surprising that someone can just call himself an analyst and start being one, but the process I went through—my own lengthy psychoanalysis—is the best qualification for helping others, short of receiving help from Christ. I was eventually to take some graduate courses in clinical psychology but to conclude that these hadn't the foggiest relevance to counseling people.

Really, I felt guilty the whole time (I was an analyst for some two years at that point in my life) for not having the standard pedigree. But I knew from getting the clients of psychiatrists and psychologists around town that I was as good as they were when it came to helping people. I got so many clients from one particular psychiatrist that I came to name their malady "the Dr. Hill Neurosis" and figure out a cure for it. Dr. Hill had managed to make people sicker than they were when they first came to him for help at thirty dollars per hour.

I didn't know exactly *how* I was helping my people, but a good percentage of them seemed to feel better and better. I simply listened to their troubles—listening can cure plenty, but it takes a lot of giving—and then taught them what Homer had taught me.

My best experience was with a girl named Mary, who was dying. She had terminal asthma, a painful way to go. Mary sometimes just couldn't breathe and her doctor and medicine expenses ran about equal to her rent. I had been treating her brother, a homosexual for whom I did little good, and I had some insight into what in that family was making everybody so sick.

Mary had been advised that her disease was incurable and she had decided to try analysis as a last resort. She came in asking for hypnosis.

I didn't know a thing about hypnosis but Homer had done some on me with good effects. I never went into a "trance" or even fell asleep, but I did get a euphoric sensation from it and a desire to speak freely. Homer had told me that the important thing about hypnosis was to act as though it was absolutely effective and to give the client perfect confidence that it would work.

"You came to the right place," I told Mary. "I'm an expert hypnotist and you're going to be asleep in three minutes. Lie down on the couch."

I didn't believe a word I was saying. But I talked softly to Mary, as Homer had done with me, and in three minutes she was sound asleep.

I got scared. I said, "Can you hear me, Mary?" She said lethargically that she could. I said, "Fine. We're going to get rid of that asthma. Tell me what's on your mind."

Mary recounted long pleasant stories about her childhood and she seemed to want to "unload." I got the feeling that no one had ever asked her about herself and, in the relaxed state of hypnosis, she was glad to have her chance.

She was a "stiff" person, by Homer's description. She walked carefully and sat upright in chairs. She spoke with clear enunciation and moved her hands very precisely in her gestures. I had come to associate this with "inner secrets" or repression. I felt that Mary had a stormy life going on inside and it never had its chance to come out. It doesn't sound very kosher scientifically, but I felt that Mary couldn't breathe because she was "full" inside. Homer concurred on that. (Homer always advised me about my clients during our training sessions. He was able to infer tremendous truths about people just by the way they sat in the waiting room turning magazine pages. I would describe my clients' revelations and Homer would propose methods.)

I began to probe Mary with questions about possible problems. Under hypnosis, such matters come out readily. Mary didn't have any "horror stories" to tell but she did mention a very early sexual experience that was typical of little children experimenting. After I woke her at the end of the session I brought it up.

She couldn't remember the details she had given, and in a conscious state she could barely recall the incident at all. But from that session on, she began to get well.

As we went along I did some input. I told her she was attractive and intelligent. She was disturbed, in her sleep, by this. She didn't *want* to be a valuable person, I gathered. I pressed the point, making sure that my compliments were an important part of each session.

I wish there were space for more details, but suffice it to say that Mary was well, completely cured of all asthma, in six weeks' time. She stopped her doctor visits and her medicines. I checked back with her six months later and she was still fine. The asthma had gone on for eight years. The cure took six weeks. The medicine was self-love.

I didn't start thinking I was a miracle man, however. I had plenty of clients who just went along with no noticeable improvement. But I quit my musical career entirely and gave my full time to psychoanalysis.

There were more "good cases." Robert, who had migraine headaches, came to me for six months, lying on the couch and telling terrible hallucinations about people wanting to kill him, his little daughter in a casket, ghosts, etc. I got so depressed and so bored that I leafed through magazines while he lay there in hypnosis. I just couldn't listen after a while.

I began calling Robert "Bob," and I told him to quit saying that he was seeing a "doctor." He had a bowing, obsequious manner that he thought befitted a Mexican-American but I told him it was a lot of malarkey. I sat there for something like fifty sessions, acting as Robert's garbage disposal, but I noticed that as he emptied his mind he began to straighten up in his posture and to speak more decisively.

There was a breakthrough in that case, too. A terrifying war experience came out from under all that Robert had stored "above it" in his mind. Robert had been in a position where people *were* trying to kill him. One day I said, "Bob, the war's been over for years. You might as well give up the headaches."

It was a shot in the dark but it worked. Robert was not so dramatic a cure as Mary—from time to time the headaches recurred—but over a period he came completely out of it. Most important, his personality became one to respect. He was straightforward and quite independent-minded after all.

Missy was an ugly girl who got beautiful in psychoanalysis. I mean really *ugly* to really *beautiful!* I have no idea how that happened. She became a totally different person. Her friends hardly recognized her. What she said under hypnosis was so commonplace that I don't remember any of it, but I was almost sorry when she went off to get married.

Buzzy was one of the most sensitive and intelligent people I ever talked to, though he couldn't read or write. He was a stone mason, and a good one. He wouldn't consider hypnosis and he acted very suspicious of me. Whenever I said anything

that sounded glib he would say, "That don't get it!"
I had to be very careful.

He came to me just after Christmas because of
terrible marriage problems. He had bought an expensive watch for his wife for Christmas but he
hadn't included a Christmas card. She had cried
about that and he was exasperated.

"Why in the world didn't you get her a card?" I
asked him in our first meeting.

"I can't read," he said slowly, watching to see if I
disapproved.

I just said, "Okay, that's a good reason." I convinced Buzzy to learn to read and I put him with
another of my clients who needed somebody to
teach something to. It was slow going. I was seeing
Buzzy's wife at the same time and trying to get her
to take it easy with him. She was a high-strung
person.

Buzzy began carrying around hunting and fishing magazines, mostly for his image, since he
could read only a word at a time by then. He looked
at my loaded bookshelves in the office one day and
said, "I wouldn't be able to understand those."

I said, "I wish I knew more about hunting and
fishing but I just haven't got your background."
The subtle competition between us was easing off.

One day I told him forthrightly, "Look, quit trying to be inferior all the time. I'm a fake
psychoanalyst. At least you're a real stone mason."

When Valentine's Day came around he asked me
what he should get his wife. I told him it was his
problem. I wondered what he'd actually get her.

At my group therapy just after Valentine's Day
Buzzy and his wife seemed very close. I asked her

in front of everyone what he'd got her for Valentine's Day. She started to cry for happiness. She told this story:

"He came home very late. Almost midnight. I was mad as could be until he gave me my present. It was a Valentine's card."

"Just a card," we all said.

Buzzy cut in, in his slow drawl. "Well, I got off work at five and I went to this drugstore where they had lots of cards. I wanted to pick the right one for her but it took me all night,'cause I still don't read so good."

"He read every card in the store," the wife said through her tears. "What a wonderful gift!"

Times like those made my career worthwhile, but it still wasn't what I wanted. I really no longer had the deep unhappiness I had experienced in music, but life as a fake analyst seemed like a blind alley. For one thing the professionals, the Ph.D's and M.D.'s, had so little talent for analysis and counseling that many people got turned off. Their high fees gave the process a bad name. I liked money as well as the next guy, but how could I help people if I drove them broke?

Homer was always hounded by associations of psychologists or marriage counselors or psychiatrists, presumably out of envy of his high client load or his skill. He charged less for better work, and that always turns off the establishment. I was frustrated.

There's a story about the guy who was "unhappy and frustrated" when he went to an analyst. After the cure he was "happy and frustrated." I was that guy.

I had started a doctorate in music before I left school to play in the orchestras. I decided, for want of anything better to do, to go back and finish it. I resolved to take graduate psychology courses just in case I got interested in counseling again. I constructed a weird program that allowed study in both music and psychology.

The university was for me, as for so many others, a good hiding place from life. It would take care of me, loan me money and feed me, and I could act irresponsibly with impunity. I could chase girls, stay up late at night, march in demonstrations, etc. Music on the doctoral level didn't require much study at all—just kowtowing to the faculty. Psychology is a weird tongue; once learned it was just a matter of speaking the gibberish back at the high priests.

The year was 1968. I was thirty and still didn't know what I wanted to be when I grew up. But right in there somewhere, I think that God began really to guide me. Because despite my intentions along the lines of music and psychology, I rapidly became a writer.

5
Love Story

"What can you say about a twenty-five-year-old girl who died?"

And then was reborn. And then witnessed to me. And finally married me.

But I'm getting ahead of my story.

First I became a writer. This happened in connection with my reviewing campus concerts for a local newspaper. I had done this work during my master's program earlier and was rehired when I returned to the university. But this time, somehow, everybody began reading my column and talking about it. I received promotions. I think God became very active in my life at that point, three years before I met him.

As my doctoral studies went on, an opening eventually developed in the university news bureau for a cultural editor. This job entailed covering various artistic programs on campus—concerts, plays, museums, etc.—and writing up news releases about them for area newspapers. I was appointed to the position.

The thing about "news" releases that bothered me was that they were biased. Since the university supported the news bureau, we were supposed to make the university look good. This wasn't too hard to do since the university looked pretty good artistically anyway, but it was a far cry from my other role as a critic, where I was able to voice my candid opinion of things.

I began to miss the clout I had as a reviewer. I wasn't really a smart-aleck critic, but I did regard as precious my right to voice a negative reaction when it was justified. It was never justified at the university news bureau. I just kept pouring out the good news. Of course I had no inkling that God was keeping me in a training program to pour out the real Good News one day.

I tried to keep my job as a critic going in the local paper but a unique situation developed. When a concert was coming up I promoted it in a news release from the bureau. Then I attended the performance as a critic. Inevitably, it developed that in my role at the news bureau I would urge my readers to attend a certain performance, and then later I would criticize that same performance in my role at the local paper.

People started catching on.

The news bureau told me in no uncertain terms to give up my critic's job but I just couldn't do that. Instead I took a pen name, Philip Levy, and continued my reviewing in secret. This became quite a joke at the local paper where they delighted in putting one over on the university.

Philip Levy got tracked down, though, and I became Mark Louis. Soon I was Lutz Rath, Jay Fishman, and a whole bunch of other people. Rath and Fishman were real people, so the news bureau had more trouble figuring out that I was the real writer. I got my friends to agree to let me use their names, and they all became "distinguished critics" overnight. But pretty soon that fell through. After all, when you've spent the evening with Fishman at the movies and then see the next morning that he has reviewed a concert, you get a bit suspicious.

I parlayed this game into a career of being other people. I began to write for a conservative magazine in a neighboring big city under still another pen name, and for a radical campus underground paper under another. Occasionally I took opposing views of the same situation.

Those were the days of campus demonstrations and inflammatory issues on the social ethics scene. I was having a bang-up time being different people with different views. At the height of all this purple journalism I wrote under eight different names.

Looking back at it I find it dishonest, as I see things now. But I remember my mood about the world then, and why I pursued such a peculiar employment. I thought life was meaningless, so why not have fun with it? I was fascinated with a quote I picked up somewhere, "Life is inexplicable, boring, and dangerous."

My studies were disappointing, as I have indicated. I disliked the strange rituals of cramming in somebody's prejudice and then vomiting it back on examinations. I lost interest even though I finished all the courses for my doctorate. When it came time to write the dissertation and take the final exams, my tolerance of irrelevance was at an end. I quit.

The Lord seemed to have something to do with that. I believe he was influencing me all along in that period: my realization grew that the world was no place to look for happiness. During my earlier times in music and in the clinic I had assumed that I was merely in the wrong work, that if I changed my career I would be happy. But I changed my work radically, and nothing happened. I still had that pervading sense of frustration and emptiness. There was nothing in life I couldn't say "So what?" to.

I knew from my own psychoanalysis that I wasn't in all that bad shape. I was a little different, but I wasn't nuts. The problem, as I now know, was spiritual. I could never have gotten satisfaction out of having a doctorate, or out of any other worldly pursuit, and I thank God for that. I would have gone on, stupidly, trying every kind of career and recreation, to the end of my life. I would have never been at peace.

But God sent his disciple Yvonne.

On February 20, 1971, the news bureau assigned me to cover the Metropolitan Opera Regional Auditions being held on campus. And there I saw Yvonne.

My first glance at her was fatal. She was just walking through the lobby of the auditorium and I thought, "If I had a girl like that, I'd really be happy!"

And for once I was right.

But of course I didn't realize the life-changing events that had to precede it all. I was just looking at a beautiful woman going by.

An hour later I was seated in the balcony writing

down the newsworthy events of the audition. It wasn't a particularly intriguing assignment. Young, hopeful singers would come out onstage one by one and sing an aria. The judges would rate the singer and somebody eventually would win the prize. I didn't know it at the time but Yvonne had twice previously been a winner in this competition.

I turned my head, looking over the crowd in the balcony, and there was that marvelous face again. Yvonne was sitting a few rows behind me in the second seat off the aisle. My heart started to beat uncomfortably and I had a fleeting thought that I might die in my chair from seeing such beauty. The person next to me knew her and gave me her name.

I pulled myself together and decided to approach her. Between singers I jumped up and walked back to her row. I leaned over the person in the aisle seat and whispered to Yvonne, "Hi, I'm Zola Levitt and you're Yvonne Golden. I think we should talk."

She was a bit stunned, but I insisted on standing there and making conversation, even though the next aria was about to start. The individual in the aisle seat was uncomfortable, caught in the midst of a budding romance.

Yvonne said something like, "Talk about what?" but she was glancing around embarrassed. People were shifting in their seats, disturbed by this impromptu conversation in the midst of their reverie over the operatic arias. I took full advantage. "We'd better go out in the hall," I whispered loudly. This seemed to satisfy the onlookers and they all looked at Yvonne as if to encourage it. She shrugged and got up.

In the hall I tried to be casual, explaining that I was covering the event for the university news bureau and generally assuring her that I wasn't dangerous in any way. I kept smiling and being matter-of-fact but I has having trouble putting words together while looking at that face.

I somehow talked her into having a cup of coffee with me after the audition.

Over coffee I told her that she was the most beautiful woman I had ever seen. She replied calmly, "I try to do what Jesus tells me to do."

Oh, no, I thought to myself. *What a waste! Such a beauty!*

I didn't know precisely what a Christian was, in those days, but in my mind I lumped Yvonne in with a general group I thought of as "repressed." I told her, "Well, I'm interested in all kinds of philosophies. I think religion is a heavy burden that people carry for nothing, frankly, but I'd like to hear your story."

We spent the rest of the evening together. I thought Yvonne was really taken with me but in reality she felt called upon to witness. This discrepancy in viewing our relationship was to surface very quickly.

I felt she had depth and she was certainly a good listener. We talked about religion and people and I ended up spelling out my general discouragement with life. She seemed to understand that and I gave her credit for having a lot of smarts.

I saw her every night for a week. Then she threw me out of her life.

She said we were getting nowhere; that there was another, entirely different side of things I didn't comprehend; that my concept of a love relationship was far from hers. She said she wished I would give serious thought to all we'd said about Jesus, but until I did, there was no real purpose in our seeing each other. She was crying.

I said that she was acting crazy; that Jesus was a great man but had died 2,000 years ago; that she just had to have some other reason for wanting to discontinue what seemed to be a growing relationship. But it was no soap.

I decided to swear off all religious nuts from then on.

Inside of me, I really did respect her. Grudgingly I had to admit that she valued herself highly and that her faith was an admirable thing. Perhaps I was actually envious of it.

And I was fascinated by her attitude. It had been a long time since a girl had looked me in the eye and told me I wasn't worth much—something I professed to believe. Her honesty impressed me.

I was able to stay away only two days.

I came back unannounced—just knocked on her door and strolled in. Caught off guard she revealed in her manner that she was glad to see me again. I went through my prepared speech: "I miss you very much. Whatever the terms of this relationship must be, I'll accept. If you want to talk about Jesus, that's what we'll do. I'll listen with all I have."

Underneath it all I may have been coming back for just that purpose, though I'd have called it by another name. What I was hungry for was "spiritual quality" and I wasn't finicky about the particular sect. Yvonne had plenty and I wanted to stand in the light. It wasn't so much a hunger for God *per se,* as for something better than what I'd found in the world. I didn't know what I wanted to eat, but I knew I was hungry.

I told Yvonne that I was lonely and discouraged, and that her company made these feelings abate. She listened with great sympathy. It felt good.

I outlined the events of my life for her, in a repentant way. I more or less "confessed" that I had run myself into a rut and that I was out of ideas.

She counseled me, according to the gospel, and she had great power. No one can oppose purity, humility, and self-esteem. Her calmness soothed me and the simplicity of her counsel—based squarely on the simplicity of the counsel of our Lord—made a deep impression. I realized how ridiculous I must have sounded back at the beginning, telling her that she was missing something in life.

She asked me to go with her to the Campus Crusade for Christ meetings. I found them rather tedious, but that atmosphere of calm and peace was in those people too. They weren't my kind of people, that was for sure. I came from loud-talking Jews who wore their feelings on their sleeves and I wasn't accustomed to the mannerly, quiet style of the CCC evangelists. I'm still not, but with spiritual maturity comes tolerance.

I mischievously determined to undermine the serenity of those good soldiers of Christ. I took every opportunity to discuss life-styles with them. I had a morbid interest in sin, it's fair to say, and I thought I could trip them up on that topic.

That was a mistake. They were innocent people, ten years my junior, and not at all informed about symphony orchestras, psychoanalysis, and all the rest of the jargon I threw at them. But I was missing the big issue.

They were hearing me out, in prayer, trying to help me.

How patient they were! I would invite the campus director to lunch and fill his ears with my worldly achievements and understandings, and he would duly give me credit, all the while probably wanting to yawn in my face. I would tell him, "You people don't know anything about sin, so how do you suppose God gives you credit for avoiding it? You couldn't get into it if you tried. You don't know enough about it!"

"Oh, I don't know," he would say. "I suppose we don't really have that big an interest in it. The Lord seems to do a lot to keep us in more profitable things."

Yvonne wanted me to read the Bible and recommended the Gospel of John. I told her I would study it but that I might find discrepancies in it. I set about trying to fault the Scriptures.

That was another mistake.

I was overwhelmed by the Gospel of John. Thrilled, convicted, and deeply moved. I realized at once that this wasn't ordinary writing, that its effect on me was mysterious. I didn't read it fast, but rather savored it.

I found in Christ an extraordinary character who could not be faulted. He was potent and stirring and definitely real—since his character was well beyond the powers of mere inventors. Jesus Christ can't have been "made up" because his style, his force, and his ideas are beyond human imagination. None of the supermen of fiction hold a candle to him. None of the great philosophers dare address his topics nor attempt such magnitude. None cut through to the heart like Christ.

I had known Yvonne only three weeks but I was spending most of my time on the intriguing topic of Christ. Every night I would take up the Bible and meditate until late. It was on one of those nights that I saw Jesus.

Finally, a few weeks later, Yvonne took me to her church. It was a big church with all the trimmings: a fine choir, gorgeous surroundings, and a minister whose "invitation" could charm the paint off the walls. When he asked for people to come forward after the service and give their lives to Christ, I had to hold onto the arms of my chair. I just refused to be psyched into it. Instead, I resolved to hang around afterward and buttonhole the minister. I thought that I could maybe find some flaw in him and deliver myself from my terrific desire to go to the Lord.

No such luck. The moment I started to talk to him I could feel that same uncanny serenity I had sensed in Yvonne and the Campus Crusaders. It just knifed through me every time like a pain. The painful part was plainly, "He's better than I, and I'm beginning to know why."

I involved the pastor in a discussion about evolution and he patiently gave his views. But there was a twinkle in his eye I was afraid of. He finally let me have it: "You didn't come to me to talk about evolution, did you? Aren't we here to talk about you?"

I shook his hand, told him he led a very nice service, and ran for my life. For some reason I just didn't want to meet Christ right then and there, but I knew I was licked.

That night I got into my armchair in my bedroom, took up the Scriptures, and started to study. But I knew there was something to take care of. I needed to interview the Lord himself. I nerved myself, and addressed Jesus Christ.

"Dear Lord," I began, in the manner I'd heard Yvonne do, "are you really there? Is there a God? I have to admit, Lord, that I haven't made anything satisfactory out of my life. Oh, it's okay, I'll muddle through. But I know there's something, Lord, that I'm not getting and not understanding. There's got to be more than this. There's just no reason for all this life to exist the way things are. There's got to be something more!

"Now, Lord, you said, 'I am come that they might have life and have it more abundantly.' That's quite a mouthful. How could you say such a thing? It gets to me, Lord, because it's just what I need. I don't need more money or more pleasure or more health—I need more 'abundance.' Something doesn't feel quite right.

"Lord, if you're there, you know what they've been telling me—that I'm to repent. Well, if you're there, you made me and you know me, and you know I'm not a very repentant type. But I *can* say this much, Lord—if there is a God I need him. I really *am* sorry for the way things are with me and I need your help.

"So, Lord, if you're there, show me."

It wasn't much of a "salvation prayer." It wasn't

what Campus Crusade told people to say at the big moment. But if you're not honest with God, where are you after all? It was the real me talking, expressing however haltingly some faith in Christ.

That's all it took for the thief on the cross, and that's all it took for me.

They say you don't necessarily experience an emotional reaction when you're saved, but I did. My life changed from then on. I felt tremendous elation as I went to bed. It was the first thing I thought about when I opened my eyes in the morning. I am saved! I'm a Christian! I'm with Christ!

I had asked him to "show me" and he did.

From that moment on, I never had to wonder if he was there. My life changed so suddenly and radically that I literally was a new person.

6
"Who's Going to Witness to the Beards?"

Two weeks later I began sharing my new faith. Not with friends and family, but with some tough customers.

I went to Daytona Beach, Florida, with Campus Crusade for their annual witnessing to the drunks on the beach during the college spring vacation.

Daytona, Ft. Lauderdale, and other vacation spots had become popular with campus "swingers" during their spring break. They came from all over the country for a week of ribald drinking and partying each year at this time, and Campus Crusade joined them on the beach.

Daytona has to be seen to be believed. I don't know if they do now what they did then, but I'd never seen anything like it. Tens of thousands of laughing, swaggering, drunken youngsters were cavorting about the streets and hotels of the little town in a nonstop bender of booze, dancing, and sundry carryings-on. The streets were mobbed with revelers day and night. Shouting and rock music never let up.

Into all that came the Campus Crusaders with

our little yellow booklet that tells how to receive Christ.

I was amazed by the whole thing. I didn't have the slightest confidence in the Crusaders; I thought they'd get laughed off the beaches. And as for the party people, deep in my heart I wanted to join them. I had spent most of my life trying to qualify as a genuine swinger and in some inner part of me I suppose I felt as though I could still make it.

Not that I was fooled by their horsing around. I knew very well what loneliness comes out of desperate partying. But in some way it seemed a lot easier than witnessing for Christ.

We were issued little wrist bands that identified us as Campus Crusaders, and they came in very handy. Occasionally the cops would raid a drunken brawl and haul everybody off to the cooler. If a Crusader was in the group, trying to share the faith, he could obtain release by showing his wrist band. The police had seen in years past that Campus Crusade was "clean," so far as drinking and vandalism were concerned.

One of our members was offered forty dollars for his wrist band by one of the swingers. It was like a credit card for breaking jail.

Crusade would not have ordinarily taken along a new Christian for such a mission, but I told them I felt "led" to go. (I was beginning to learn the Christian language.) Actually, I did feel a tug to get out into the field and try my new faith, but the main issue was that Yvonne was going and I couldn't have gotten along without her for a week.

The Crusaders, about 750 of us, were put up in neighboring hotels, and we walked together each morning to nearby churches where we received some Bible teaching and some words to the wise about witnessing in these circumstances. I found the Bible teaching fascinating but I had my objections to some of the attitudes about witnessing. "Girls, don't be caught alone with any of those guys out there," one speaker exhorted. "They're monsters! They're animals! Take one of our guys with you at all times!"

"Now just a second," I whispered to Yvonne, "they're not animals out there. Aren't we supposed to love them? I thought they were just people in need."

Yvonne told me that the policy of the organization was not to witness across the sex line. Girls didn't witness to guys and vice versa. I just stared at her for a minute and she finally thought about how I had gotten to Christ. If it hadn't been for her, I would probably have never taken it seriously. In my newfound erudition I lectured her on how our Lord had witnessed to the Samaritan woman.

I thought that Christians weren't meant to be an elite group on earth, looking down their noses at the lost. But I must admit, the speaker might have a good point in a practical way. Once I got out among the teeny-weeny bikinis on the beach I almost forgot what I came for.

Then Lee came on the scene.

Lee was a wandering vagabond, to look at him. He was tired, unshaved, and dressed in army fatigues. He wore a pack on his back in which he carried his worldly belongings. I found him walking down the street and I attempted to witness to him. He said he was a Christian already and he needed a room for the night.

I got Crusade to put him up in the room where I was staying, which made a total of six guys in one room. But, as things went on, we were honored to have Lee among us.

He was a true apostle. He simply traveled around the country, thumbing rides and preaching the gospel. The Lord fed him and clothed him, as he did the birds and the lilies. Lee was a Jewish Christian with an intense sense of mission. His faith was deep as the ocean. He didn't work and he didn't worry about it. He was only interested in directing people to Christ. He amazed me.

When we got up the next morning I asked Lee if he'd show me how he witnessed, and I skipped the morning meeting of Crusade. Lee was one to get up slowly; he rolled around in his sleeping bag for about an hour, gradually coming to life while I paced around the room. At length he sat up and got out his pocket-size Bible and began to study. He lit up a smelly black cigar.

I told him I wanted some breakfast and I said that we weren't getting anybody to the Lord sitting around the room.

"All in good time," he chanted, seemingly entranced by the Scriptures he was reading. "The Lord is already up," he assured me, "and he's already bringing us someone to cleanse."

I began to think Lee was plain crazy.

Finally, laboriously, he got to his feet and got dressed. It was about 10 A.M. We went down to the hotel coffee shop where Lee ate the biggest breakfast I ever saw one man consume. He lit up another

54

of those cigars and said, "The Lord is our shepherd."

"Let's get down to business," I said. I took him by the arm and dragged him out of the place. As we passed an ice machine outside, a girl's voice came down from a balcony above. "Hey, is there any ice left down there?" she called to us.

Lee looked up at her slowly and said, "We'll bring you some." She disappeared at that and we went over to the machine to get some ice. Lee said, "You see, there she is. Crying out for Christ. God sent her to us."

I said, "Come on, Lee. She's already drinking at this hour. All I heard her cry out for was ice."

The ice machine was empty. Lee paused for a moment and then gave it a tremendous kick with his boot. It shuddered for a moment and then coughed up a few cubes. We found a clean white cardboard box on the floor, put the ice into it, and set out to find our Samaritan woman.

We walked along the same balcony where the girl had appeared, not knowing what room she was in. Loud music came out of several rooms but Lee, pausing at each door, was somehow able to know where we would find her. He said finally, "She's in here," and he knocked.

I was beginning to feel a little strange.

The same girl answered the door and was grateful to us for bringing the ice. She asked us in for a drink. Lee accepted the offer and I began to wonder about his motives. There we were in the midst of a party which had either started early that morning or was still going on from the night before. Girls and guys were spread out through the small room, some on the beds asleep, some on the floor, some constantly passing from that room to others along the balcony. Everyone seemed preoccupied, listening to deafening rock music. They all kept their noses in their drinks. There was little conversation.

It seemed sad. The ocean was just outside. They had traveled a long way to be at this beautiful place. But they were just drinking away their day.

Lee and I stood together, sipping some awful wine and trying to look like swingers. He was concentrating hard and I think he was talking with the Lord.

Finally he said to me quietly, "Tell them to turn off the music. I'm going to preach."

Incredulous, I did as I was told. I walked to the middle of the room, smiled at our hostess and said, "Lee, here, is kind of a traveling prophet, and he wants to say something. How about turning off the music a minute?"

The term *prophet* turned them on. They thought I meant something occult, which is endlessly interesting to the party set. They turned off the music and looked to Lee, bemused and curious.

Lee made quite a speech. "I came from Viet Nam about two years ago," he began, "and I was on the needle."

He revealed his background as a dope addict and general sinner in a quiet, sincere voice while his listeners grew more and more interested. His story was frightening in its intensity, and it made everyone in the plush room feel a bit sheepish, yours truly included.

"I was ready to die. More than ready," he said as he reached into an inner pocket for his tattered little Bible. "Then someone told me how to get to God."

I thought he'd lose his audience with that one, but nobody stirred. Lee shared Revelation 3:20, John 3:16, and other of the stock-in-trade I'd picked up at Crusade meetings. But he was no scrubbed Campus Crusader. He was obviously a man who had walked through the valley of the shadow of death, and he was here to tell about it. The party people were visibly moved.

I assumed we would be making disciples at once and I was ready to take names and addresses to send them literature. But Lee wrapped it up simply. "God bless you, every one," and he walked out. I followed right after and grabbed his arm.

"Lee! Don't you want to have them pray with us? Where're you going?"

"None of them are going to the Lord now," he said. "They'll talk about it for a while and then reject it. But the seed is sown."

I thought he was a bit negative on that. I resolved to go back to them later on. Lee in the meanwhile took his leave, thanking me for my hospitality but explaining that his real ministry was in the barrooms and jails and that he had to get going. I shook his hand respectfully. The last I saw of him was when he walked out into the street and stuck up his thumb for a ride.

It was lunchtime at the hotel and I went to find Yvonne. She was eating with the Crusaders. I told her about my exciting morning and fairly dragged her back to that party room. It was about two hours later by the time we got there.

And we found that Lee was right. They were still

discussing his talk. They hadn't turned the music back on. We found the whole group talking about God together. The drinking had apparently stopped.

I thought to myself that we were going to reap a huge harvest in that room, but I was wrong. Yvonne testified to them and I told my brief testimony of some two weeks, but as Lee had said, they all wanted to think about it some more.

"God bless you, every one," I said as we left, in the manner of that mysterious traveling prophet.

Now that's the kind of thing that impresses me. If there's no God, where do people like Lee come from? He might have been sent, I thought, not to testify to those kids in that room, but to testify to me. Deep inside I thought it was very logical that the clean-cut kids of Campus Crusade should be loved by God. They were so "all-American." But Lee was like me, a creature of feelings and moods. In all his sensitivity he might well have understood that I was a part of his mission.

In any case he really built my faith. He was worth the trip to Florida.

During the remainder of the time, two people actually did pray with me to receive Christ into their lives. I didn't really think it was possible until it happened. I'd had steady discouragement through the week, trying to talk to some really tough cases. In one case I chewed the fat with a Catholic boy who explained the essentials of his faith. I asked him, "Where do they get all that stuff? It's not in the Bible." He didn't care to look at my Bible to see if it was.

The first guy I was able to help find Jesus approached me during one of our Crusade shows. Our weight-lifting team had held forth on the beach, leaving the crowd weak with awe at their prowess. After their demonstration the athletes all individually testified to Christ. The implication was that if these accomplished men had found what they wanted in Christ, then everybody ought to buy him. It felt a little like a shaving cream commercial to me, but it actually worked. I can say as an eyewitness that many people made sincere confessions of faith in Jesus on the inspiration of those demonstrations. (My cynicism about them might have been based on the fact that I sneaked up to the weights they'd been hefting around after the show and I couldn't lift even the lightest one.)

The second guy who prayed with me was an interesting case, and he may have been the reason for my trip. He was a hippie, feeling out of place in the milieu of fraternity types and their rightful female prey. He was too far out to mix with either the townfolks or the swingers. Of all things, he ended up sort of following the Crusaders around.

Some of our group tried to witness to him but he wasn't having any. But one night he approached me and told me his troubles. He was having a dope problem, among other things, and felt generally unwanted in the world. He turned out to be sixteen years old.

I asked why he picked me to talk to and he said it was because I wore a beard. He was right: of the 750 Crusaders present I was certainly the only bearded one. He was like a gift of God to me because I wanted to prove my point to Crusade with him. As it happened I mentioned him every single time somebody criticized my beard. "Who's going to witness to the beards if you don't have me?" I would say. Or, "I'm going to introduce you to a brother in the coming Kingdom who will explain it all."

This guy wrote a beautiful poem the night he came to Christ, which I read in one of the general morning sessions of Crusade later in the week. I followed up on him by correspondence and verified that his profession of faith was real and continuing.

When I returned to the campus I felt inspired to carry on my faith-sharing mission. It's fun to share Christ. Even when the recipient doesn't show the slightest interest in the topic the conversation is invariably rich. Christ is more basic to talk about than anything else in the human condition.

I decided to go about my mission very directly. There was a pleasant grassy area on campus called Dunn Meadow, where students would hang out on nice afternoons. They lounged around on blankets, threw frisbees, played with dogs or just slept away the day, but the place was always busy. As a result many special interest groups on campus would set up makeshift booths and pass out their literature or discuss their particular cause. The campus political organizations, women's liberation, and the like made good contact with the student body in Dunn Meadow.

I figured Jesus would fit right in.

But I couldn't very well set up a "salvation booth." I had to have a gimmick.

I prayed about that and had an inspiration. I made a cross out of two rough pieces of wood about three feet high and a hand-lettered sign saying "Rap about Jesus." I went out to the Meadow by a little creek that ran through the middle and stuck my cross in the ground. I sat down beside it with a Bible.

It hadn't occurred to me until I got there that the little creek had a rather special name, for my purposes. The students affectionately called it a river and it had been named for a former university official.

His name was Jordan. I had stuck my cross in the ground beside the Jordan River.

When I got seated and arranged that first afternoon, I looked across the Jordan and saw the Palestine Liberation Front tent. My natural enemies, the militant Arabs, were passing out their inflammatory anti-Israel literature right in front of my ministry. "All things work together for good...," I thought.

The ministry was a busy one right from the start—not because everyone wanted so badly to "rap about Jesus" but because they wanted to see what sort of idiot would sit there and do that. I got into some interesting dialogues.

One boy came by wanting to debate the merits of Christianity against the Eastern religion that he followed. He felt that I was a fellow mystic, since I too believed in an invisible God, and that together we could solve this world's mysteries. He was far too deep for my new knowledge of spiritual things and I told him so. I quoted the blind man in John 9 and paraphrased, "Whether your state of Nirvana and 'being at one with your being' is valid or not I don't know. I just know I was blind and now I see."

I began to notice that people would plop down around me but not really want to discuss anything. Did they just feel good beside the cross? Inquiry showed that some were already saved but never did witness to anyone. Others just wanted somebody to sit with, and I was collecting a pretty good-sized group. Still others wanted to eavesdrop on the sharing but not get into combat over the gospel.

A big red-haired guy came over and said he was a Mormon. I didn't know what Mormons thought so I asked him if he believed in Christ. He said he did, so I invited him to sit down and share his faith. (I didn't realize, of course, that he believed so different a doctrine about Christ, but, funny thing, he subsequently came to Campus Crusade meetings with me later on. It pays to accept people as they are.)

I did all this on weekend afternoons and I found it refreshing. Nobody was getting saved that I could see, but Jesus was getting good exposure among the plain folks, whom he loved in his own earthly ministry. Everyone in the big meadow noticed my sign, and one day a guy filming a movie came over to include me as the village idiot. I suppose my cross and sign added local color to his film of the campus.

But one day I got the acid test. An Arab sauntered across the creek and stood looking down at me. He was from the PLF across the river.

He said, "Tell me something about Jesus."

I replied, "He loves you."

The Arab sat down heavily, eyeing me all the

while. Jews and Arabs know each other pretty well on sight.

He started a long story about Jesus' reputation among the Arabs of his country; that they thought he was a real prophet, etc. I was glad we were staying off politics. He concluded by saying that he personally felt there was more to Jesus than he had been told.

That set off my inner alarm and I said, "You're right about that. I don't know much about Jesus but I know he is God." And I opened my Bible.

I didn't know much about the Bible either, and I used the Phillips translation for sharing, since I could follow what was meant. I happened to open to the passage about Jesus taking the hand of the little child to demonstrate what a righteous man was. (If this sounds like amateur witnessing, it was. I didn't know enough about Christ to do anything but wholly depend on him. I hope it's still true of me.)

The Arab was mightily impressed with that passage. Somehow it was just the right thing to share with him. It wasn't the first time I had "magically" said just the right thing while witnessing.

I was still wary of my new acquaintance, afraid he was putting me on. I was prepared just to shove him into the Jordan if he gave me any trouble. He was going to be surprised at how fast we "baptize" around here.

But he was sincere. In fact, he was deeply touched. I told him, "A little child, like the one Jesus selected for his example, wouldn't know much theology. If he wanted to know Christ and follow him, all he could do was ask, in simple words."

"Yes," said the Arab.

"Will you bow your head and 'ask' with me?"

"Yes," he said, and bowed his head and closed his eyes.

"Praise God," I thought to myself. "What do I do now?"

I started to pray. "Dear Lord, I don't even know my brother's name, here, but you have every hair of his head numbered. You love him, and you died for him. He wants to claim you and have his reward. Come into his life right now...."

I waited, holding my breath, to see if my Arab friend would join in. After a long pause he said simply, "Yes."

I said "Amen" and we opened our eyes. I told him, "Your troubles are over."

He walked away, back to that tent.

Will I see him in the Kingdom? In his way of putting it ... "Yes."

And that was the only guy in the whole of my "Dunn Meadow Ministry" that ever bowed his head and prayed with me. Did God send me out there to help one Arab? Why not?

I tried sharing the faith with everybody else I knew, of course, but it didn't go so well. At the news bureau where I worked, the cigar-chomping reporters thought I was a nut. I ran into old friends and they thought, "What next?"

I began to feel uncomfortable in my own habitat. I'd had a great spiritual awakening and I wanted to proclaim it to the world, but I wasn't taken seriously. It began to get my goat. I asked the Lord to accept my application for Christian work.

There was one hope for this. During the Daytona trip I had become acquainted with one of the Campus Crusade leaders who was working on Explo '72. Explo, a projected 100,000-member evangelical conference, was to be held in Dallas in June 1972. Somewhere during the spring of 1971 I wrote to him and asked if he needed a writer.

I didn't really want to leave Yvonne or go to Dallas, but I felt "called" to do something for the Lord. It was a profound feeling. I came to see that my worldly work was useless—day after day "managing the news" to make my university look good in the papers. In the meantime the majority of the people in the world were suffering along with no spiritual side to their lives, in much the same miasma I had formerly experienced. I wanted to share my new life with them.

My new life in Christ was just that, a "new life." It's impossible to explain to unbelievers and too obvious to explain to Christians so I'll just say that he keeps his promises.

So, in faith I applied for Christian work.

Explo '72 was in fact in great need of a writer of news releases since they planned to start promoting the gigantic event a year ahead. But they weren't ready to hire a new Jewish Christian, sight unseen. The Lord provided a way.

I was invited to attend Campus Crusade's Institute for Bible Study (IBS) being held that summer of 1971 in Dallas. The SMU campus was made available to Campus Crusade, and this would give me an opportunity to visit the Explo offices across town while I studied in the Institute. That way they could look me over and try me on some assignments before committing themselves.

I bargained for an extra long vacation from the news bureau and they agreed to let me have the time. But I would lose my pay for the period. The IBS lasted six weeks. I had only two weeks of vacation coming.

But it seemed as though the Lord was taking a hand in things and I decided to go anyway. It must have been a testimony at the news bureau to see an editor sacrifice four weeks' pay to study the Bible.

In faith I set out to become a "professional Christian."

7
So Who Needs Money?

The Institute for Bible Studies was a strange experience.

It seemed to be divided about half and half between studying the Bible and studying how Christians are supposed to behave. It really served as a kind of boot camp for Campus Crusade, imparting the peculiar, highly-disciplined life-style required by that organization. A fascinating course on the Book of John was juxtaposed with a Sex, Love, and Marriage course, and I wasn't too certain of the connection.

Also, I was rather out of my element. I was booked into a dorm room with a young fellow from Chattanooga and I spent most of my evenings conversing with fraternity men and football players from southern universities. (Other IBS locations in other parts of the country would also have been attended by those close to the respective area, but of course I chose Dallas because of Explo.)

The student body of the IBS were mainly undergraduate college students, less worldly but more spiritually experienced than I was. I began to feel like a loner, unable to make real contact.

At the same time some of the teaching irked me. Naturally the Sex, Love, and Marriage course was designed for those with little dating experience and lots of life ahead of them. I had lots of life behind me. I got bored on the one hand and rather cynical about the advice-column atmosphere on the other.

I suppose all this just proves that a thirty-two-year-old can be an intolerant and immature Christian. All the same, in my own Christian walk I have always been more of a yielder than a self-accomplished saint. I would rather give my troubles to the Lord and let him take care of the perfecting than adopt some ideology that's supposed to keep me out of trouble. One man's opinion.

The Explo headquarters was a different story. I enjoyed the energetic atmosphere and prayerful confidence of the Crusaders who intended to host mighty Explo '72. They had achieved miracles already, for instance in the equipping of their office, which was in an old house. They prayed for carpeting and carpeting came. They prayed for typewriters and typewriters came.

Actually, Christians around the town had responded to their requests, but remarkable stories abounded of how people got impulses to help out. Some equipment turned up completely unsolicited. Dallas was obviously proud to have Explo '72 in town.

I wrote two news releases which met with approval, and I talked at length with the executives about what contribution I might make to the effort. They were trying to determine, in prayer and in their own minds, whether I was a man sent by the

Lord, or just a man looking for some adventure.

At length we agreed that I would go back to my old job for the remainder of the summer and meditate about the Explo possibilities. On their end they would also be in prayer. We would maintain a correspondence and I would advise them from a distance about the press and media department.

That accomplished, I turned my full attention to the IBS courses. But I really was discouraged. I began to realize that I was just plain unable to sit still in classes and study for exams any more. Ten years of university life had burned me out completely.

What I liked better was one-to-one discussion of the Scriptures, an old Jewish tradition that was in my blood. I would always try to corner somebody with questions. The faculty responded well to my curiosity, while the students seemed to think that asking questions was sin.

At the end of the third week I quit. I called home and told Yvonne to fly down to Dallas and drive back with me. I missed her so badly that I just couldn't face the drive without her.

When she arrived, my fellow students were surprised by her. They had been surprised to learn that I worked at the Explo office, they were surprised that I composed Christian songs (which they enjoyed singing), and now they were surprised that I had a "standard brand," highly spiritual, Christian girl friend. The bearded stranger was full of surprises!

I didn't really "walk out" on them. I explained that I was losing weekly paychecks and if I were going to work for Explo I needed to save money.

That much was true, but I think they realized I wasn't happy. Nobody was really at fault except maybe the great doctrine of conformity. If an individual doesn't quite fit with the group, something goes wrong. I still experience the feeling of not fitting in with Christian groups, and it's caused by nothing spiritual but by the fact that I'm Jewish, bearded, and inclined to be independent.

None of those are "un-Christian" in themselves. (All were true of our Lord, I gather.)

People ask me why I just don't shave off my beard and avoid looking different. Well, besides not caring to avoid looking different, I have my own reasons. I actually prayed about this on several occasions but things seemed to happen that justified my beard. First, of course, was the kid in Daytona who was able to approach me because I wore the beard. I'll see him again in the Kingdom to come, and if I shave it off he may not recognize me. Then, during the Explo year I went to a news conference where Billy Graham was appearing. While we newsmen were firing questions, Billy looked at me and said, "I was jest admirin' thet beard! It's a beauty." Maybe he was just showing the newsmen that he was tolerant, but I like Billy Graham and I respect his opinions.

And then there's the whole matter of sharing Christ with the Jews. To the Jews a beard is holy (Numbers 6:5). It has always been the separating mark of the devout believer in God among the Chosen People. Believe it or not, it still makes a difference to the Jews. Even my mother likes it.

When I went to the Wailing Wall in Jerusalem I noticed that the worshipers stood aside as I approached the Wall, giving me a place of honor right against the stone. My appearance impressed them that much. (They would have been horrified if they'd heard my prayer: "Thank you, Jesus, for preserving your brothers and mine, and regathering us to our land.")

Finally, Yvonne liked my beard and that settled it.

Despite the news about my leaving IBS early, which must have traveled to Explo headquarters across town, Explo got in touch immediately and I served as an out-of-town advisor during the summer of 1971. The media department would write or phone and I would give opinions or dictate news releases to be processed in Dallas. I deeply respected them for the fact that my difficulties at IBS didn't seem to bother them.

I was in prayer, in the meanwhile, about finances. Campus Crusade members lived on a draw account kept at their central headquarters and supplied by contributions from their churches or wherever they could raise support for their ministries. They drew about one-third of what I was used to.

And I now had my son to support.

I'm sorry to drop that like a bomb, dear reader, but that's how it happened to me. During my time at the news bureau, my ex-wife was killed in an accident. The custody of my son, Mark, now nine years old, reverted to me.

That was before I became a Christian, and I had wondered at the time I received Christ whether God had called me because I needed him in trying to be a father. I was having a tough time as a single parent with a full-time job, though Mark always was, and always has been, delightful company.

Mark received Christ on his own shortly after I did, and I must say it made a difference. We became a happier pair.

So it was Mark and me together deciding if we could go to Dallas and live like Campus Crusaders on the pay of one devout college kid. Mark was eleven during that summer of 1971.

I finally relented, convinced that this was the call of the Lord, and I told them at Explo '72 that I wanted to come on full time. I asked for a financial consideration for my son, and for the fact that I couldn't raise money from any churches because I didn't belong to any. (I wasn't against churches per se, but I wasn't well enough acquainted with any to ask for money from them.)

Explo was very generous and provided us an apartment along with the salary a married Campus Crusader would draw. We figured we could get by. Our income would come to around $350 per month but we would be doing the Lord's work. It was a far cry from playing $100-per-day Glen Campbell Shows but I was pleased to be called.

I had an interview with my managing editor at the news bureau before I left, and he was highly skeptical. He was an "unsaved churchgoer," a kind of individual who is able to understand the sentiments of the Christian but has no appreciation of the power of the Lord. He felt glad that I'd had a spiritual awakening in my life but he thought I'd starve to death working for the Lord.

He was wrong.

This matter of sacrificing for the Lord is tricky. In

a way it can't be done. Whatever one sacrifices one gets back, I've found. Money given up for the Lord comes roaring back overwhelmingly. Sin relinquished makes the heart free for greater joys. Time given to his work brings rest and peace. The replacement of worldly knowledge with study of the Scriptures brings wisdom.

It seems obvious, but few really take a chance with the things they hold dear. I'm one of them who is too careful. I've had the striking experience of giving up income, first two-thirds and finally all of it, and have seen the Lord support me and even provide abundance.

But other little behaviors in my life are not pleasing to the Lord, yet I hang on to them as if they were more precious to me than God himself. The Apostle Paul had the same problem. He wrote of doing what he wished not to do and vice versa. We are amazing creatures, stuck in our flesh but bought with blood to be freed.

Don't read on for an answer to that one. I don't have it. I'm only saying that where I have had faith in my God, I have prospered.

If this helter-skelter story about one stumbler tells you that, I've achieved my purpose.

8
First-rate Santa

Explo '72 was a conference, or a gathering, of 100,000 Christians (at least as advertised) in Dallas in June 1972. The number 100,000 was to be raised by the various Campus Crusade members on their college campuses. They exhorted the multitudes to register for the conference and get themselves to Dallas and participate. It wasn't just a single meeting but rather a week-long succession of huge meetings, based on the subject of how to share one's faith in Christ with others. The delegates to the conference, all 100,000, were to go to morning and afternoon sessions in which they were to study the Scriptures and ways of witnessing. And then each evening the entire membership of the conference was to be gathered in the Cotton Bowl, a gigantic football stadium in Dallas.

And it worked out pretty much as planned. There weren't quite 100,000, but it was close. And the people were somehow accommodated with places to sleep and eat. Many Dallas homes were opened and hotels were booked full. The various classes and sessions and maxi-sessions in the Cotton Bowl came off pretty much as planned.

There was also a long-range objective for Explo: to evangelize the entire United States by 1976 and the whole world by 1980. The thinking was that if 100,000 Christians could learn successfully to share their faith in one place, at one time, with a uniform strategy, these could then go out and disciple others. And there was a direct plan that each person there would disciple five more by the end of the summer following Explo. Then in the fall of '72 there would be 500,000 expert evangelists in the United States and in the countries represented at Explo, which were quite a few. This army would go forward sharing the faith, heavily in the United States and in the other countries too. By 1976 the United States would be completely evangelized, and by 1980 the world. (By "evangelized" Campus Crusade meant that the population would be told the gospel, not that each one would be saved. Campus Crusade was aware, as the rest of us are, that the majority of the world will by no means be saved at the end times.)

It was a mighty ambitious project, and a very worthy one as far as I was concerned. The gifts I had already experienced by the time I went to Explo, when I had been a Christian just a matter of months, had convinced me that what the world needed now was Christ. (I still feel the same.)

You can imagine that assembling 100,000 mostly college-age people from the United States and several foreign countries, into a city of 800,000 for a whole week, was quite a task. It required more than a year of planning, and the Dallas headquarters where I went to work was the center of this huge operation.

My job was to write news releases about what we were up to and issue them to newspapers and magazines nationally to keep the name "Explo '72" before the public, and to continue reassuring readers that it was all going to work. The news releases were a way of getting publicity in faraway places and of informing the public, those interested in it as well as those indifferent to it, about what we were trying to do.

I reported to my supervisor at the office on the appointed day and set to work. I enjoyed the atmosphere. The office was a friendly old house, with not more than a dozen or so people working on the project at that time.

My supervisor was one of the most amazing things about Explo to me. He was my introduction to Bible doctrine, a disciplined life, total commitment to Christ, and a virtually fanatical devotion to sharing the faith.

His name was Dan and he was a law graduate from the University of Texas. He had planned to go into politics and he was well suited for it, being a handsome, pleasant person with a good mind. But Christ had turned him around in his tracks, and he now devoted himself to the penniless pursuits of Explo '72.

He read the Bible day and night. I never saw a man act as a director of media communications, planning a conference involving 100,000 delegates, and still read the Bible while he worked. He had a huge filing cabinet of Christian doctrines gathered from the Scriptures and from commentaries, all typed out with references and all pertaining to how to live this life in the Lord. He was an expert on Scripture and seemed to have the answer for every question in life.

I liked him, though sometimes I thought he was crazy.

Driving anywhere with him was quite a nuisance. No matter how late we were or how crucial the time factor, Dan never broke the speed limit. No matter that the newspapers provided a pulling-up spot for cars dropping off news releases; Dan always parked in a parking lot because he thought it wrong to obstruct the street. He eschewed evil.

If you've ever worked for an office issuing news releases to daily newspapers, whose presses are ready to run and whose editors are hurtling frantically from room to room, you can appreciate how it felt to drive there at twenty-five miles per hour and then search for a parking lot when we finally arrived.

Dan was an absolutely tireless worker. He arose every morning at five for Bible study and his own prayers. He was always the first one at the office. I could see by his work that he would sometimes beat the eight A.M. starting time by two hours or so. Yet he held Bible classes every evening, or shared the faith, or went to church. I asked him one day if he ever went to the movies and he said he didn't. I asked him if he thought movies were sinful. That was beside the point, he said. He thought wasting time was sinful. I said, "Aren't there some really edifying movies?" Dan said, "Garbage in, garbage out." He meant that movies were "garbage," and that if a person put garbage into his mind, garbage would come out of his mouth.

This phrase fascinated Mark, my son, who went

around quoting it gleefully when I explained its meaning. To Dan it seemed that everything outside the service of God was garbage. I didn't agree with this, because of the simple fact that we sometimes don't realize when God is working through us. Sometimes in the course of daily events, when we carry on secular work or play, we find chances to witness, and people are saved. Suffice it to say that I have seen people saved at the movies.

Mark started to attend Dan's evening Bible study for children. Dan would drive through the city, no matter what distance, pick up everybody's children, take them to someone's home, and teach them the Scriptures patiently and accurately in a language they could understand. I was very grateful to Dan for this. Mark got a solid grounding in the Gospels and a highly accurate picture of our Lord.

In fact, Mark went on to hold his own children's Bible study in our apartment complex. I was immensely proud of him and impressed with his doctrine. Mark taught a rather hard line of repentance for salvation, not out of line with John the Baptist's message, and he brought little children to the Lord according to the Four Spiritual Laws of Campus Crusade. Once while eavesdropping from the next room on his Bible study I heard him going over the principles of salvation with a four-year-old girl. She had apparently come to the Lord the week before, but Mark didn't seem satisfied with her testimony. So he took her through the Laws once again and she listened carefully. At the end of that she said she felt completely saved, and this time he was satisfied.

Mark didn't shirk witnessing to adults either. On one occasion I remember him coming into the house kind of glum after failing to bring to the Lord a man outside working on his car engine. I explained to him about seed sowing—that this man might later come to Christ on the strength of the things Mark had taught him, plus new experiences of a spiritual kind in his life. But Mark has Jewish blood; he likes to close the sale at the time of the demonstration.

At the office Dan was a heartless taskmaster without appearing to be so. His example of constant work without pause, without rest, without fatigue, was downright obnoxious. And it wasn't as if he realized that he was a little special in this way. He thought everyone was made just like him in regard to their zeal for work, that anyone relaxing must be ill or caught up in sin. Like many other of the male staff at Explo, he failed to notice the women working in the office. He was kind to them and even chivalrous, but he never had a date and never cared to. He felt he was called to a ministry of being single in order to carry out his total commitment.

He lived at home with his parents, ate there —except for his lunch which he brought to the office and ate while working—and he never indulged in entertainment of any kind. I tried to fault him in all this; I teased him in good humor, and he returned only kindness. I ended up like the fellow in the poem "Gunga Din," saying, "You're a better man than I am."

The Explo headquarters in general was a much more disciplined, tightly-run ship than the secular newsroom I had come from. The peculiar practices of the organization were in full force: supervisors could not be criticized or questioned in any way, weekly reports had to be submitted by each worker telling what he had done with his time in the office and at home, women were invariably given subordinate roles, and a standard operating procedure was established for virtually everything. I wasn't comfortable with this, but I have to admit that it brought results.

The place seemed to me to be like a military base, but it was at a military base that I had first seen the interesting motto "If it works, don't fix it."

I must say again, as I have all along, that I was the peculiar one. I couldn't have started some kind of freethinker's revolution at Explo '72 because I couldn't find anyone else in the office who really sympathized with my view of the thing. I would take my complaints to Dan very often since he was right across my office, and he would give me consolation and tell me the scriptural support for some of the practices done in our routines of work. But it was often suggested that I had a critical spirit and this was not a good thing in walking with the Lord.

On the other hand, people sometimes said that I was a breath of fresh air.

In any case, the work went along and I enjoyed myself very much. Explo was a pleasant thing to promote. Newspapers seemed to receive the releases eagerly enough and we had pretty good press play around the nation. Once in a while an editor off someplace in Montana or Kentucky or Florida would start running everything I sent and would really catch fire.

Of course we prayed about these things and expected that they were an answer from the Lord. Registrations for the great event were pouring in as early as the winter before, and we kept getting new personnel in the office to help us handle those. Our little company kept growing.

There were a great many good times, of course. I made many friends among the workers at Explo, and we enjoyed Bible studies and evening get-togethers. I especially remember the Christmas party held by the staff; it was my first Christmas as a Christian.

I was raised in a Jewish home and we didn't celebrate Christmas other than for the wonderful increase in business it brought to my father's store. My father had a 5 & 10 that sold Christmas ornaments and toys, and of course we considered it a merry time of year without its spiritual significance. What a friend we had in Jesus!

Christmas mornings I would go to my Gentile friends' homes and see all the presents they got, and so forth, but in a way they didn't impress me as much as they would someone whose father didn't have a toy store. I was in on the whole deal. The way they were bought, the way they were wrapped: all that was no mystery to me. As you may suppose, I didn't believe in Santa Claus. But this Christmas at Explo '72 was different.

Christmas of 1971, I, Zola Levitt, played Santa Claus for the Campus Crusade Christmas office party.

My beard was simply irresistible to the female staff, who thought they could decorate it with some sort of white, powdery cosmetic. They made me up a first-rate Santa suit. Children who saw me in my full regalia took me for the authentic Saint Nick.

As Santa Claus, of course, I had the honor of handing out presents to everyone at the party. We had arranged beforehand that everyone would draw a name and would then bring a present for that person. There were many gaily-wrapped gifts.

Into our party there somehow strolled two small children, two little Mexican boys who lived in the apartment complex and were attracted by the lights and the noise. And, of course, the appearance of Santa Claus. We invited them in, naturally, and the girls hustled off to a corner and made them up presents after learning their names. When the big moment came I included them with the other names I read off, and they each received a present. They were amazed by the whole thing.

When we prayed afterward, someone said, "Dear Lord, you said, 'Suffer the little children to come unto me,' and we thank you for bringing us children tonight."

When I came to the present for Dan, I called out, "... and this one to Dan, from a secret admirer." It brought down the house. Dan's face got red.

Sometime around that Christmas I was approached by the father of one of our workers with a manuscript that he wanted made into a book. He said there was some interest in it from a publisher and that he just needed the writing straightened up and made readable so he could submit it. He naturally approached me since I was sort of the house writer. I said I'd be delighted to do it, not realizing at the time that this quiet event really amounted to

God's call to me to become a writer of Christian books.

During early 1972 I worked that manuscript over, and it was accepted by the publisher. And I said to the Lord, "Why can't a fellow just sit down and do *that*? Why does he have to come to an office every day?"

Needless to say, I was spending a lot of time writing letters to Yvonne, talking to her on the phone with my usual expensive lack of restraint, and thinking about her day and night. I had been pestering my bosses to hire Yvonne, and I knew that if they provided her work on a Christian project she would relocate to Dallas. And I knew that she wanted to be with me. I had managed to bring her down for a weekend visit during the fall so that the people at Explo could talk with her and see that she was kosher. I tried to give the impression that if only my girl friend were in town I'd settle down and be a real member of the organization. I was in constant prayer about this and so was Yvonne. And finally, just before the first of the year, she came to Dallas and joined our headquarters staff.

When I met Yvonne at the Dallas airport (called Love Field, incidentally), it was as if I'd never seen a woman before. I had the experience of Adam when he was suddenly given a helpmate. It wasn't that I couldn't remember what she looked like. She just looked *so good* to me. To let my heart stop pounding, I sat her down for a cup of coffee in the airport before taking her outside.

I think it was at that time that I decided there was no way through this life for me without Yvonne.

But I didn't realize what a long time marriage would be in coming.

Yvonne settled into the office perfectly. She was an ideal Explo '72 worker and seemed to notice none of the things I complained about. People couldn't understand how we fitted together. (They still can't.)

I got her settled with a roommate in the same apartment complex where Mark and I lived, and we rode together to work each day, ate lunch together, and rode home together.

You'd think with all that I could have gotten the lady to marry very quickly, but Yvonne was circumspect. I think she thought I was a little crazy.

Explo moved its headquarters to a new building which had been donated or given for the interim, rent-free or something—we never heard, other than that the Lord had answered our prayers. I liked the old house better. Actually we had swelled up to two old houses and I liked each of them better than our new modern office building. It seemed cold and official. It had white walls, tile floors, and very few windows.

Through the spring before the conference, my work started to deteriorate. It usually does each spring. News releases were beginning to get me down. I had been in the business of promoting institutions and events too long. I was just about "promoted out." Yvonne was no help to my work. The combination of spring outside and her somewhere in the building made me restless at my desk.

I remember having long conversations with the Lord. I would ask, "Why isn't it fun, Lord? Why doesn't your work make me feel spiritual? Why does it end up feeling like the same old newsroom? Why can't I get convinced that we're going to evangelize the United States by 1976 and the world by 1980? That's what I'm in charge of telling others.

"Why don't people really love each other, Lord? You commanded us to love one another, but we don't do it, Lord. We mouth it, we give it lip service, we obey an ethic called Christianity, and, yes, we even put ourselves out and try hard to think of the other fellow. But why don't we really love each other?

"Dear Lord, I feel very lonesome."

This wasn't an easy time for Mark, who has been a cheerful child from the day he was born despite a life with some heartbreaks. But Explo almost did him in. Naturally he was in a new city and a new school, and my own schedule didn't permit us very much time together. The Explo day had swelled up to seven A.M. to six P.M., and I would come home very tired. We would have supper and then I would want to see Yvonne. I had to divide my time between Yvonne and Mark very carefully so that the two people whom I really did love would feel taken care of.

It is clear from Scripture that God knows every moment of our troubles and trials in this life, and that for believers all things work together for good. I didn't doubt for a moment that what I was experiencing was for a purpose and I tried hard to determine that purpose.

Now, with hindsight, I see God's purpose in it for me. I wouldn't have had the guts just to drop out of the workaday world and give myself completely to

God, unless I became so discouraged that I almost didn't care what happened to me. When my work at Explo was done I didn't seek another job at all. I had managed to save a little bit of money from the publication of that book I mentioned, and I had about one month's living expenses available to me.

I said to the Lord, "If the lilies of the field are arrayed better than King Solomon and the birds of the air get their food, why do we have to work, Lord? If money is something the Gentiles seek, I'll stop seeking it." I earnestly believed that the Lord would take care of me. I thought that I could write another book and that I could write enough of it in a month to interest a publisher. And then I could ask him for an advance big enough to live on for the next month, and so on.

It was a perfectly crazy idea. Although I didn't know it at the time, the average publisher takes only one manuscript out of each 200 he receives. Self-sufficient authors, those who earn enough by writing books to make their living, are extremely few. And I was completely a beginner. My only experience with a book was the editing I had done on that prewritten manuscript, so I really didn't know how to begin.

In prayer, I sat down to write *Satan in the Sanctuary*.

9

"I'm Going to Starve to Death."

Satan in the Sanctuary, which turned out to be a best-seller, was not originally my idea. It resulted from a short article brought to my attention by Dan in the Explo office one day.

The article was written by the Rev. Tom McCall, a missionary to the Jews, whom God seemed to appoint to be my next teacher in my Christian walk. I was fascinated by Tom's article, which appeared in *Bibliotheca Sacra*, the scholarly publication of Dallas Theological Seminary. It wasn't the subject matter—the "tribulation temple" possibilities—that got to me; it was the Judaism. The way Tom wrote, the history and future of the Jews seemed important to Christianity.

I had thought my Jewish days were over when I received Christ. Like so many other Christians, I thought I had now become something very different from the Jews. Little did I realize that my true understanding and appreciation of the Jewish faith were about to begin.

The Lord took a hand in bringing me to Tom McCall. Part of our Explo promotion was done by film-screenings in local churches; the film urged church members to register for the big event. As a routine assignment I drew Tom's mission house, "Beth Sar Shalom" ("House of the Prince of Peace"). I thought that while I was there I would question him about his article, and particularly about Hebrew Christianity, whatever that was.

The mission sanctuary was quite different from the churches I had attended. As a Jew I felt comfortable there. And well I might; the room was designed with just that in mind. It had subdued lighting, dark wood paneling, and a deep rug. A Torah (the Hebrew scrolls of the Books of Moses) and a Menorah (the candelabra) graced a front mantelpiece. There was no cross or baptistry or other Christian symbol. The synagogue-like decor was meant to bless the Jews, in accordance with God's recommendation.

Tom was a pleasant, soft-spoken, ministerial type, with an enormous knowledge of Jewish history, culture, and custom. He told about his lengthy and peculiar education. He had a secular degree, followed by a master's and a doctorate of theology, followed by the intensive study course in witnessing to the Jews given by the American Board of Missions to the Jews (ABMJ). Since his Th.D. was in Old Testament studies and his missionary training emphasized Jewish traditions and "styles," the Scotsman McCall was one of the most interesting "Jews" I'd ever met. (He ate pickled herring in sour cream at home.)

The folk who attended the friendly worship services at Tom's mission house were an odd lot. Some were lifelong Christians with a burden for Jews. Some were Hebrew Christians, who have burdens enough already. Some were unsaved Gentiles who slipped into the worship at the House of the Prince of Peace because anyone was welcome and there was no pressure.

And finally there came the whole point of the matter, a precious few unsaved Jews.

I think most people came for the same reason that I started to worship there. The place was warm, the door was open, the company was terrific. It remains my favorite church home.

Tom gave me to understand that I was a Jew and a Levite and that I could stand tall with Jesus, my brother of Judah. He said that Jews made fine Christians and always have. He mentioned a few: Matthew, Mark, John, Paul, Peter, etc. He asked if I realized that Jesus is Jewish.

That much I realized but it had never made much sense to me. I had appreciated that our Lord's personality, as I appraised it from the Gospels, reflected a Jewish "type," but I had never understood the orderly progression of God's chosen men. Jesus is identified in the opening statement of the New Testament as "the son of David, the son of Abraham" (Matthew 1:1).

"Aren't you, too, the son of David and Abraham?" Tom asked. Something happened in my heart then. I suddenly realized, all in an instant, that God's special Covenant with my people had never been broken. It had been extended to the Gentiles by a gracious God—well and good—but it had never been taken away from my people. They need only their Messiah.

I can't tell you what it meant to me.

As my Explo year went on, I became active at the

mission. I acted as the music man, organizing a choir and playing the piano and organ. Eventually I started to speak in churches as a representative of the mission.

I started really to study the Old Testament, a rather rare pursuit at Explo. Only Dan seemed knowledgeable about the things Tom had told me, and he backed them up 100 percent. (One day I asked Dan what he did for excitement in his life and he said, "I read the Old Testament.")

When I stopped my Explo work and "dropped out" of the salaried world, the first place I went was the mission. I asked Tom if he thought God would support me and he said he thought he would. He said that I ought to feel "called" to do what I was doing, however, and he asked if I had any plans. I told him I planned to write books. Fast.

And so we took out his interesting article.

I won't go into what Tom said in his article, since *Satan in the Sanctuary*, which was based on it, is available. In brief, Tom thought that the "tribulation temple," the third Temple of Jerusalem, was in the offing in Israel, and that its construction would set off the "end times" events.

We prayed together about writing a book, and we set to work at once.

We finished off three chapters in as many weeks and sent them to Moody Press. Tom and I waited for a reply, Tom hoping for the chance to extend his mission to the Jews by this, and I hoping for my rent.

But publishers are extremists. Either they want a book at once—"yesterday," as they say—or the months drag on and when you call they say "Zola *who?*"

I said to God, "What did you get me into here? I'm going to starve to death!"

But God answered my prayer in his characteristic way, just when I thought he'd failed to post my rental deposit. Tom Goode called. Goode was a retired pro football player, the center for the Baltimore Colts in his last season. I had met him in the course of writing my first book, which I've already mentioned. That first book, *Somebody Called 'Doc'*, was the story of the pro football chaplain and his peculiar ministry. I had met a number of the pros in doing my research, and had even sat on the bench for a game.

Goode said he was going to be in Dallas and wanted to talk about having a book written about his life and ministry. I jumped at the chance. Tom was a good center, a good Christian, and a person interesting to me because of his background. He was born and raised in the woods of Mississippi and had quite an original view of things.

He had a Will Rogers-like drawl and a slow, gentle way of putting things. Combine that style with a man of monstrous proportions, who broke chairs when he sat down, and you have a unique evangelist.

He asked what it would cost to have a book written and I told him I really didn't know. He was, in effect, my first customer. I told him I assumed that God had brought him along and that I intended to charge only what I needed to live for God's work. I figured that I could write his book in something like one month, so I charged what Mark and I needed to live on for a month, $500.

And I made a contract spelling out that he was to recover his $500 from the book sales. In that way I was really not charging anything; only asking for a loan to live on while I worked.

I'm not boasting about what a fair guy I am, but trying to emphasize that I really believed the Lord would take care of me. He has and he always will. I still write my books under the same understanding.

I arranged with Goode that I would travel over to Mississippi to see his home environment. I would stay in his home with his family for one week, interviewing him and looking through his old football scrapbooks. That, I figured, would be enough time for me to get the material. I would then spend the next three weeks in intensive writing and finish the book.

I'd had good training for speedy, accurate writing. Back in the newsroom I faced many a situation that called for it. "Levitt, get me a story on the new opera in twenty minutes." "But chief, I haven't even seen that opera." "That's nineteen minutes now!"

In prayer, I went to Mississippi, knowing that God had seen to it that I'd had the necessary experience for the job. We wrote the book in seven days. I don't know how it happened, but I prayed each morning when I awoke, and I was able to sit ten hours a day at the typewriter. I didn't get tired, and the writing seemed to be up to par. In fact, it was taken by a major publisher by return mail.

I originally called it *God's Servant Goode,* but it came out as *Guts, God, and the Super Bowl.*

That really convinced me I had read correctly the will of the Lord for my life. It didn't promise financial security but it showed that I could do it. And I had survived three months without a job. (At this writing, it's getting to be two years. The Lord is a reliable employer.)

You may wonder, "What did he do all day? Did he sit around killing time?" That's pretty much it. As an author I wasn't in terribly great demand. Yvonne had gotten a full-time job in Dallas after Explo, and I did a lot of sitting around. But I was thinking hard, and I needed to.

I wish I could tell you I spent long hours studying the Scriptures, but actually I played the piano, went swimming, and kept up a running conversation with God about what was going to happen to me. Mark was getting paid off for all the time his father was out working, and I thanked God for the opportunity. My son and I had loads of time together.

I was always in a little panic to get something to write, but you can't just walk up to people on the streets and ask them if they'd like to have a book done about themselves. In a way I wish I could. I read somewhere that "some people write great novels ... all of us live them."

But I figured that if everybody in the world had a story to tell, only God could select which ones I should work on for his purposes. And I left it to him. It wasn't that I didn't have my weak moments. Sometimes I felt like a bum, having so little to do with my time. Sometimes I felt as if I should go out and get work, at least for appearances. But I had made an agreement with God and he had held up his end of it. Even if I was feeling broke and restless I was going to wait for his call.

When I had already spent Goode's money and there hadn't yet been a reply on *Satan in the Sanctuary*, I lost my grip. One day I went outside, looked up at the sky like Tevye in *Fiddler on the Roof*, and told God, "What a fine mess you've got me into. You said, 'Be it unto you according to your faith,' and you know very well I've been hanging in there. Now I don't have my rent and it's the second of the month!"

I stood around accusing God for quite some time. I thought he was very impractical, preaching the Sermon on the Mount but leaving me without my rent.

On the way back in, I checked the mail. There was a huge check, the advance for *Satan in the Sanctuary*.

I stood there looking at it, stunned and embarrassed before God. It was much more than I needed. My cup ran over. I spent the rest of that day meditating on Mark 9:24, where another confused father pleaded, "I believe. Help thou mine unbelief!"

The thing that amazed me about myself, during these long months of solitary self-examination, was that I could hang on to a little bit of doubt no matter *how* much God sustained me. I'd had some remarkable answers to prayer during that year but I still couldn't keep from thinking that God would forget me.

My abscessed tooth was a case in point. It had

come to me during the spring of my Explo year—a big, painful swelling on the right side of my gum that had me seeing stars. I remember driving along in my car and telling God, "Now you know I don't have time for this. Dear Lord, you touched the lepers and they were healed. Please take care of my tooth."

And when I returned to my dentist the abscess was gone. He asked me what happened. I told him. He got out his original x-rays of my mouth and stood there scratching his head. He kept asking what happened. I kept telling him. He wasn't a believer, but he got a lot closer to God that day.

But even on something like that, my unbelief would horn in. I would think, somewhere in my doubting heart, "If I have faith in some kind of supernatural power, it can cause chemical changes in my body."

Once I was very late for an orchestra rehearsal (I would, from time to time, sit in with community orchestras to keep up my playing), and the oboe player (that was I) can't sneak in late. He sounds the A to tune the orchestra. I had about twelve minutes to drive ten miles through heavy Dallas traffic. I sent up a quick prayer about it, ordinary situation that it was, and I made the rehearsal on time. Every traffic light turned green just as I approached it and the traffic kept moving fast.

But I remember thinking afterwards, "Oh, well, if one drives the same route time after time, sooner or later all the lights will be green." I just didn't want to give God the credit.

I have a feeling that it's part of the human condition to resist overexercising the faith muscle.

The thing to be learned, as I discovered, is that God seems to reward even the slightest demonstration of faith. I was offering faith no bigger than a grain of mustard seed, but I had the assurance that I could move mountains. Like my friend Tevye, I was convinced that no matter what happened to me, God was on the job in my life.

In the fall of 1972 I started to write magazine stories. I hit on a few of them and the payments kept us going. Tom was kind enough to dream up every sort of writing assignment for the mission and he gave me a lot of speaking engagements. I also wrote two "private" books, for a local evangelist and a pastor, which got us through two months of expenses. The private books, as I thought of them, were not for general publication but just to be used in the ministries of two men.

It's just so much bookkeeping if I go through each project that came by, but suffice it to say that through the fall of 1972 and the following winter God sent enough for me to continue my full-time writing ministry.

It wasn't really abundant. One night I was invited to an autograph party for a fellow Hebrew Christian writer and I couldn't afford to buy his $1.75 book. It looked terrible, as though I were jealous of him and refused to support his ministry. I even mumbled an apology to him that I didn't have that much money that I could spend, but I don't think he believed it. Soon after, another author who was at the party sent me $50 in the mail. I used it gratefully (it came in the nick of time again) and returned it the following spring when I was more flush.

Yvonne auditioned for the Dallas Civic Opera and made it into the chorus. I was very proud of her and I took her along on my speaking engagements to sing for the folks in the churches. She confided in me that she enjoyed singing "Amazing Grace" in a little church on a Wednesday night more than performing *Pagliacci* for a crowd of 5,000 at the opera.

I could sympathize. In my time as a conductor I had performed in white tie and tails for huge audiences, all the while thinking, "What's this all about?" But I had no such cynicism in the Lord's work. I never considered my writing to be anything but a sanctified activity, and even now I get more out of it than I used to get out of all that fuss in the concert halls.

I struggled through the winter and the beginning of 1973, but March was a very bad month. I had to sell our piano to make the rent. I said to God, "Why take my piano?" It was an old upright that I'd bought for $60 and tuned myself, and it didn't bring much. I certainly missed it.

But had I been able to foresee all that was coming I wouldn't have minded a bit.

At the end of March, when I was so broke that we weren't going to have enough food, let alone rent, I placed an ad for some marriage counseling clients. This sounds like secular work, but I promised myself that I would witness to each and every one of them. I could only assume, by the way it came about, that the Lord wanted me to do it.

Witnessing while counseling takes God's help. It's no good, of course, to tell an unbeliever that Jesus is the answer when the unbeliever has come for scientific counsel. Psychological counseling always has to have some medical mumbo-jumbo about it to make it look first-class, and people actually respond better when they think the counselor knows a lot of therapy terms.

I developed ways of making them ask me what my personal "secret of success" was. (The counselor always gives the appearance of being a more successful liver of life than the client, and the client typically swallows it whole.) When they asked I would say, "Well, I started to read the Bible about two years ago and it worked wonders for me." This, coming from a coolheaded psychological counselor made them more curious than if it were coming from an evangelist. It kind of sneaked up on them.

Sometimes I would bring it up. "Let's look a moment at a successfully lived life. Take Abe Lincoln, or, say, Jesus. Now Jesus gives us quite an example of maturity and self-esteem. And he indicated, in his wisdom, that all of us could do what he could do. In fact, he said we could do even greater things than he did."

When Jesus is approached as an example of "success," people get interested. If I found the client picking up on what I was saying I would recommend some reading in the Gospels. It's remarkable how up-to-date and pertinent the Gospels really are. Few unbelievers realize that fact, and it testifies to them.

Sometimes I had to leave it alone, of course, but I never did that without saying, "It works for me."

When I would have the kind of client burdened down with sins, real or imagined, I would read the passages about the adulteress, the thief, etc. People worried about security would get my personal favorites, the birds of the air and the lilies of the field.

I would often have to water down the spiritual message a little for starters: "Let's look at the Bible, as a collection of man's wisdom...." But I sowed a seed at every opportunity.

The Lord blessed. Some people were saved, and I got my living for two months.

But then they suddenly stopped coming. Nothing would help it. They just quit coming and no new ones called. My practice died off as quickly as it had started. I wasn't at all discouraged because I was in fine tune with God and I knew something was coming. But in my most earnest prayers I still didn't realize what surprising things God had in store for me.

I was to go to Israel in the service of the Lord!

The galley proof, the typesetter's copy, of *Satan in the Sanctuary* had come to Tom and me, and we got a call from Mal Couch, a distinguished evangelical film maker. He wanted to see the galley. He was interested in making a movie about the Holy Land.

We couldn't believe it. Apparently word had gotten out that our book was going to do well, and Mr. Couch was interested. His firm, Evangelical Communications Research Foundation, is based in Dallas, and Tom and I hustled right over with our galley.

Mal doesn't sit on things very long. Within a week he called us in with finalized plans. We were all to leave for Israel in four weeks. I was to write the script. Tom was to be the technical consultant. And I was to appear in the film.

My Jewish looks, beard and all, were paying off again. Now I was a "movie star."

10
A Levite at the Wailing Wall

Before I received Christ I had little desire to go to Israel.

But now my excitement over the chance to go to Israel was so intense that I fell to my knees. I told God, "Dear Lord, if it isn't going to happen for some reason, let me know it soon. I don't want to hope too long."

It was my time spent at the mission and the patient teaching of Tom McCall that gave me my knowledge of what a Jew was. In my youth I had spent seven years in Hebrew School and ten years in Jewish Sunday school. (The Jews had Sunday school on Sundays so as not to defame the Sabbath.) But in all that study I had not learned what a "chosen person" was. I had not clearly learned that God had chosen my people. I had not, in fact, learned that there really was a loving, responsive God.

When I became a Christian I realized that God is alive and well and thus his choosing of my people really meant something to me.

My European refugee Hebrew teachers had drummed into me a heavily accented Hebrew so that I sound as though I were born in Poland when I speak Hebrew today. They had taken me through my Bar Mitzvah—the celebration of a boy becoming a man when he reaches thirteen years of age —and they had instilled in me a reverence for God. They had taught me to cover my head and to speak to God in the ritual prayers they thought he preferred. But they had not made me feel loved by themselves or by God, and they hadn't even mentioned the possibility.

McCall, on the other hand, whose excellent Hebrew was peppered with the accents of modern Israel and who could have read the Old Testament with the best of my teachers, showed me God and showed me love.

I was so excited about Hebrew Christianity, or Messianic Judaism, or whatever you prefer to call it, that I started a book called *Jesus–the Jews' Jew*. It has now been released. It tells everything that I learned from McCall: about Passover in all its Christian splendor, how the various Jewish feasts reflect our Messiah, and the fact that Christianity used to be Jewish. (Funny, it doesn't *look* Jewish.)

When McCall taught me how to demonstrate the Jewish Passover in churches, I was stunned to find that I and all the other Jews who celebrate Passover faithfully each year have always honored our Messiah, Jesus. During the Passover service the Jew takes a piece of matzah—the unleavened bread, striped, pierced, and pure—wraps it in white linen, and "buries" it out of sight for the duration of three cups of wine during the service. The hidden piece of unleavened bread is brought forth at the drinking of the third cup—called "the cup of redemption"—and everyone takes a piece of it with a little wine. I was amazed to see that the Jews were observing Communion while they celebrated Passover, and the Christians were celebrating Passover while they observed Communion. People worshiping can't help becoming "one in Christ."

This is a long topic—the spiritual connection between Judaism and Christianity—and deserves a book by itself. It is enough to say that never before in my life had it been so significant to me that I was Jewish. How I looked forward to seeing my promised land!

In the spring of 1973, Mark turned thirteen. Like any good Jewish father I arranged for his Bar Mitzvah. I conferred with Tom and we planned a Hebrew-Christian Bar Mitzvah. It was to be an opportunity for sharing the faith in Christ—the testimony of a brand new man. We scheduled the first Sabbath after my son's thirteenth birthday to devote the mission service to this great event in his life.

The mission folk came out full force and were joined by other of my friends and a number of curiosity seekers.

Some people in the congregation had come because they wanted to see what an authentic Bar Mitzvah looked like. The one they saw was the most authentic, from God's point of view, that they would ever see!

The American Bar Mitzvah boy normally reads from the Scriptures and then gives a speech in English about his convictions on this singular day. I wrote a speech for Mark that expressed our views as Jews, as Levites, and as Christians.

On the day before the big event I got out my hair-cutting tools and prepared to work on Mark's prodigious mop of blond hair, as was my usual procedure. But he prevailed upon me, on the grounds that he was about to become a man, to have a first-class professional haircut.

I took him to a friend of mine who has a shop and got him the full treatment, including shampoo and styling. Never did anyone leaving a beauty shop look more like a man!

And so the following evening, decked out in his finest double knits, the gleam from his hair fairly lighting up the sanctuary, my son Mark nervously took his place at the podium. Tom gave a brief introduction explaining what a Bar Mitzvah was and then called me to the front. The multitude gathered in the House of the Prince of Peace stirred as I took off my prayer shawl and draped it over my son's narrow shoulders. I placed my own skull cap ceremoniously on his head and returned to my seat. I sat there a little shakily as my son prepared to speak.

I had drilled him carefully on his Hebrew, probably imparting that Polish accent to the next generation as we went, and he was able to pronounce his formidable full name expertly.

This is what Mark said:

> I am Mayer Eliezer ben Zelig Fivel Halevi—Mark Louis, son of Zola Phillip, the Levite.
> And today I am a man.
> This is my Bar Mitzvah. Bar Mitzvah means "Son of the Commandment." Today

is the Sabbath following my thirteenth birthday, and I now take my place as a full-fledged member of my tribe. My father, and his father, and their fathers' fathers reaching back thousands of years to the time of Moses, were members of the great tribe of Levi.

Today I am not only a man, but a Levite.

Today I am a priest.

The Torah—Book of Deuteronomy, chapter 10, verses 8 and 9—gives the very special will of God for my tribe. The Hebrew tells us: *Boas hahi hivdil adonai es shevet halevi losayn es aron b'ris adonai la-amod lifnay adonai l'sharso ulvorayk bishmo ad hayom hazeh. Alkayn lohaya l'levi haylek v'nahalah imehav adonai hu nahalaso ka-asher diber adonai eloheka lo.*

In English this means, "At that time did the Lord separate the tribe of Levi, to bear the ark of the covenant of the Lord, to stand before the Lord to minister unto him, and to bless in his name unto this day. Therefore there was not assigned unto Levi any portion of inheritance with his brethren: the Lord is his inheritance, as the Lord thy God hath spoken to him."

My forefathers were therefore separated as a tribe to minister to the Jewish people and to bless them in the name of the Lord. They became the high priests of Israel, as God willed.

The Levites stood as God's representatives on earth, going among his chosen people. They prayed for the people and exhorted them to greater faith. They carried out the sacrifices in the mighty temple of Jerusalem. They set the stage for the coming of the Messiah, Jesus Christ.

My ancestor Jesus was not of the tribe of Levi. His tribe was Judah. Revelation 5:5 describes him as "The Lion of Judah."

It was God's will that his Son come as a plain man, an honored son of Judah, but not a high priest. In fact, it was my ancestors of Levi, at the time of Christ, who were unable to recognize their true high priest—the ultimate fulfillment of their millennia of sacrifices and priestly works.

But it is my privilege today, at my Bar Mitzvah, to honor Jesus, my brother of Judah, the Son of God, the King of the Jews. I am a Christian.

Although I am today a priest of Israel, I serve a higher Priest. Although I am a man today, I serve a better Man. I am the son of a Levite, but I serve the Son of God.

It is still, in our time, not understandable to many Christians that Jesus Christ was Jewish. He is as Jewish as I am, and as my father is. He came to his own and they rejected him, but he is to reign in the future on the throne of David.

Only a Jew may sit on the throne of the great King David. Jesus was thoroughly a Jew in his earthly ministry. When he had only a few hours before his crucifixion, he sat down with his disciples and celebrated Passover. In the Book of John, chapter seven, we see him making a dangerous and secret trip of 100 miles on foot to celebrate the Feast of Tabernacles at Jerusalem. He told the Samaritan woman, "We Jews know what we worship—salvation is of the Jews."

What a statement! "Salvation is of the Jews." True enough, a Jew came to save the world from sin; and he chose all Jewish disciples and all Jewish apostles to take forth his message. All of the initial Christian churches were wholly Jewish.

There was a time that a Gentile-Christian was an impossibility. Today, the Hebrew-Christian, like me and my father, is quite a rarity.

But every letter of God's Word must be fulfilled. Salvation is still of the Jew.

I met the Lord Jesus Christ two years ago. Perhaps the testimony of one who has been a man only since sundown today will not be meaningful to many. But I can tell you that God is real, that he redeems his promises and answers prayer. I can tell you that I have no fear of life, and certainly no fear of death. Sin has no power over me and I stand with my Lord, my Brother, in complete confidence.

When the Lord called me I was a child. Jesus said, "Suffer the little children to come unto me." Today I am a man, but still a child in respect to God. The Book of John relates, "To all those who received him —the Messiah—he gave the power to be children of God."

To conclude this Bar Mitzvah message I would like to take this opportunity to bless you people in the name of the Lord, which is my privilege as a Levite. This is the first blessing I will utter as a man and as a priest, and I give it to you with thanks.

Please bow your heads:

"Dear God, we see in the Torah, in the Book of Numbers, that you gave my ancestor Aaron, the brother of Moses, the first high priest of Israel, your very words to bless the people. In your kindness and wisdom you have brought me to my Bar Mitzvah, and you have brought this congregation of people for me to bless.

"Therefore, in the name of God the Father, Jesus Christ, and the Holy Spirit, I, Mark Louis, the Levite, do hereby pronounce upon these people the sacred blessing of my brother Aaron:

"*Uv'rekeka adonai Veyishmereka ...* The Lord bless thee and keep thee: The Lord make his face shine upon thee, and be gracious unto thee, the Lord lift up his countenance upon thee, and give thee peace. Amen."

The congregation was very moved. The special grandeur of Jewish ceremony was mixed with the special joy of Christian worship, and everyone was smiling in fulfillment. Mark simply glowed as the whole congregation came forward to congratulate him on becoming a man.

We had some food then and some joyous singing as is the custom at the mission. But the next event was the smasher.

I had invited a friend who was an Israeli, and he came forward to ask McCall just what we were up to.

Tom resisted the urge to say, "I thought you'd never ask," and took Yitzhak to a table in the corner of the dining room. They sat down over the Scriptures as the guests were departing.

Yitzhak, of course, had many questions on just how the name of Jesus Christ got into Jewish worship. Tom had many answers. As the doctor of Old Testament studies held forth from the Scriptures, Yitzhak became a bit abrasive. "I don't really believe the Jewish Bible says that. You're reading to me from a Christian translation." Tom smiled and said, "You're right. We should get out the original." And he reached to a shelf behind him, producing the authentic Hebrew Bible as used in the synagogues, and continued to share the faith with Yitzhak from the Hebrew.

They went at it by the hour, Tom and Yitzhak, as Mark and I waited patiently, looking for any way to assist. It was nearly midnight when we left. Mark had passed the time by looking around for anyone who might want to shake his hand, and getting hugs from Yvonne from time to time. I kept a close ear on the conversation of Tom and Yitzhak, trying to look very healthy and happy even though I was a Christian, for Yitzhak's benefit.

I wish I could say that the evening was climaxed

by Yitzhak's coming to the Lord, but he remains to this day a much wiser but unsaved Jew. I remember saying to him as I left the mission, "Yitzhak, I envy you. I have a great longing to see our promised land."

All of the foregoing might impart to you just how I felt when the idea of going to Israel first came up. Only a few weeks after Mark's Bar Mitzvah the plans were made final and I was reviewing my archaic Hebrew in hopes of being able to ask for a cup of coffee in the language of the prophets.

Mal set up our trip, which included Tom and me, himself, and Jerry Callaway, a long, tall Texan cameraman. We were to be in the Holy Land some two or three weeks shooting scenes that pertain to the book *Satan in the Sanctuary* and would come out with a film called *The Temple*.

We had the assistance of a Hebrew-Christian Israeli guide, who would be able to get us into the archeological diggings at the Temple site and the Dome of the Rock, and who would be proficient to point out to us the sites of biblical significance. With Tom's expertise into the bargain we had no lack of knowledge of our filming locations. Add in me and my beard and we even had an authentic "front man." We were going to Israel and bringing our own Jew!

When the trip was completely arranged and our departing date was definite, I went to Yvonne and proposed marriage. I said, "Marry me and I'll take you to Jerusalem on our honeymoon."

She gave it some serious thought. A girl doesn't

get an offer like that every day. Yvonne certainly liked the idea of going to Israel but, as she pointed out, there was a long life to be lived after that.

We resolved to pray about it for a period of two weeks and to see each other daily and think together about this important decision.

And we found in all honesty that something wasn't quite right. Despite our prayers, despite our earnest seeking for a positive answer, something was missing. Rather than feeling the confident spiritual feelings of Christians in love, we kept getting stuck on small details and we began to quibble. At length we decided to table the motion until my return.

Next to receiving Christ, the trip to Israel was the most marvelous event of my life. From the moment we left New York on El Al Airlines until the moment we returned, I was a completely different person. I saw things I had never dreamed of. I carried a notebook through the entire trip and noted almost everything that happened to us. Eventually I made my notes into a book called *Israel, My Love.*

There isn't space here, nor even in ten books this size, to write out all the feelings I experienced in connection with my promised land. I can run over some high points in this space and say only that everyone should see this remarkable land, the promise of God, the center of the earth.

El Al is the first experience connected with Israel and a one-of-a-kind undertaking. The Israelis, who have a constant security problem, guarantee the safety of every passenger with a painstaking and sometimes very frustrating maximum security system. One gets the feeling that every third passenger on the airplane is a G-man. The sight of young men holding submachine guns in Lod Airport perfectly expresses the problem and its necessary solution.

The very first place we went in Israel was the Western Wall, called the "Wailing Wall," which is a relic of both Solomon's and Herod's great temples of the past. Here the orthodox Jews collect daily for their somber ritual prayers, pressing into the cracks of the wall slips of paper which bear special messages for God. I was thunderstruck at the sight of them. For a certain scene in our film I was provided the full regalia of a Levite and sent directly to the wall to pray with my brethren.

Everything in Jerusalem is stone, which is a matter of municipal law. The marvelous stone of the Holy Land, used by builders from King Solomon on, is plentiful, reliable, and imperishable. Walls stand in the old city from millennia past. Nearby, high-rise apartment buildings made of the same stone decorate the ancient horizon.

I had some very odd moments looking around the land that was somehow in my blood. One evening tears started to come down my face as we watched a sound and light show at David's Citadel. The narrator was speaking of the eons of time during which the walls around us had survived bloody assaults of troops of so many nations, and somehow it all overwhelmed me.

Our guide was successful in getting us permission to film the underground diggings by the Western Wall. We saw amazing sights, including the room identified as the Sanhedrin where our Lord Jesus Christ stood trial. We also saw a white-haired old man down in the caves where it was cold and damp, bent in supplication to God. He had received permission to come there every day and do his prayers at the site nearest the buried "Holy of Holies," where God dwelt in the temple.

We saw the outdoor diggings at the southern end of the temple, near the Huldah Gate which Jesus and his disciples used to enter the mount. There the excavators had uncovered the sites of the moneychangers' booths and the pavement laid by King Herod. The pavement, impervious to the centuries, was in fine shape.

We did have some difficulty at those particular diggings. When we arrived at the site, despite our government permission and letters to that effect, the reigning authority—a tough, red-headed Israeli with a pick in his hand—decided not to admit us. He looked over the group carefully, probably wondering why I was traveling with Gentiles, and I stepped forward hopefully and pronounced my name—Zelig Fivel ben Yosef Leib Halevi (Zola Philip, son of Joseph Leonard, the Levite). He seemed struck and stepped back in admiration of a Levite. "Thank you, Lord," I thought, as he waved us through with his pick.

It was fun filming the ancient sites with Mal, Jerry, and Tom. We moved fast, got a lot of stares, and generally appreciated the Lord's choice of our work.

On the Sabbath when things were quiet, Tom and I went to Galilee. Jerry and Tom took a general drive around Israel, filming sites like Masada and the Valley of Megiddo. With Mal driving, they covered almost the entire country in a single day.

Tom and I ate St. Peter's fish at the Sea of Galilee—landlocked, freshwater fish undoubtedly the same as those caught by Peter and the disciples. It was delicious. I can understand how our Lord preferred it for breakfast.

We went for a swim in the Sea and I tried to walk on the water. I did this by perching on top of a slippery rock, but after yelling for Tom to see the miracle I slipped and fell in. He asked, "Did you doubt?"

Tom had a friend in Tiberias by the Sea who took us on a tour of the fascinating local surroundings. We had lunch at a kibbutz and examined that life-style. We heard stories of Syrian invasions and constant trouble at the borders. We shared in the tribulations of those who defended the farms with bottled gasoline against tanks. We saw the rows of underground shelters where the tillers of the land were obliged to spend their days and nights during each uprising of their Arab neighbors.

During that Sabbath Tom baptized me in the Jordan River.

I had somehow not gotten around to being baptized, and I was a little argumentative about it when it was brought up. On one occasion a local church wanted to include me in a program of baptism of Jewish believers. It felt to me like the solemn ceremony was being made a demonstration for the benefit of the congregation. But under the good counsel of Tom, and in the atmosphere of green Galilee where Jesus walked, I felt persuaded in my heart and I followed the Lord in baptism. We were at the Jordan close to where it flows out of the Sea of Galilee.

Remarkably, while Tom and I were still standing waist-deep in the Jordan, an Israeli came swimming by and asked us what we were up to. He had watched our small ceremony. And there we witnessed, explaining that a Jew can follow Christ and that the Messiah himself had been baptized here. Our fellow bather, a bus driver from Tel Aviv, was nonplussed by our message. At the end he shrugged as if to say, "You just never know who you're going to run into when you go for a swim in the Jordan."

Back in Jerusalem we filmed more at the temple mount, this time in the Dome of the Rock and in the Arab quarter. We went into Solomon's stables, an enormous underground fieldhouse inhabited only by wild birds. We interviewed the young archeologists working at various sites near the mount, and got some positive opinions about the possibility of the Jews' rebuilding their own temple. This would be, in prophecy, the coming "tribulation temple."

We had a rare opportunity one day to show Mal's film *The Return*, based on Hal Lindsey's *The Late Great Planet Earth*, at the Jerusalem Ministry of Tourism. There a Jewish audience, including the Chief Rabbi of Tourism, watched the evangelical film. They complimented Mal and Jerry on doing a good job of honoring an honorable people. *The Return* describes the regathering of Israel to its land.

After the film we buttonholed the rabbi and actually tried to share the faith. He gave us a good conversation, telling the Jewish interpretations of prophecy and referring constantly to "the Scriptures," although we were unfamiliar with his references. Mal finally questioned him on chapter and verse, and the rabbi shrugged, "Well, some of this is in the commentaries." He was referring to the Jewish rabbinical teachings.

He evaded our witness with the skill of a Pharisee.

We went to the Messianic Assembly, a Hebrew-Christian church in Jerusalem, and there interviewed missionaries engaged in the difficult task first attempted by our Lord: the sharing of the faith in Jerusalem. We attended a fine Christian service where the preaching was in Hebrew, and a Hebrew message on the wall at the front of the sanctuary said, "Blessed is he who comes in the name of the Lord."

On the 9th of Av we went to the Wailing Wall. This is the melancholy commemoration of Tisha B'av. On this calendar date in history both former Jerusalem temples were destroyed: the first by Nebuchadnezzar in 586 B.C., the second by Titus and the Romans in A.D. 70. The Jews never forget the 9th of Av, the "Day of Sorrow." It was August 6, 1973, and we were there with our cameras.

On this particular festival the Jews arrive at sundown bringing prayer mats. They put these on the ground and spend the night, literally crying through the Book of Lamentations. They sob aloud with the great prophet Jeremiah over the tragic loss. We stayed with it until late at night, walking among the mourners, picking up the sounds of the actual crying for our film. It was an emotional experience for me. To give a picture of the enormity of that scene of lamentation I can mention that there were 10,000 mourners present.

I began to long for America. It was a funny feeling, as if Israel was simply too much for me. I'd had a dose and needed time to recover from it. I longed to hear American spoken, drink a glass of water with ice in it, watch a ball game on TV, and any number of the other myriad little things you give up when you change countries. The nearly 400 passengers on our returning El Al plane gave the captain and crew a round of applause when we touched down at Kennedy Airport.

I had a new perspective now, an expanded consciousness. The trip with all its mixed feelings —holiness, and hard but godly work—changed me. I had written to Yvonne from Jerusalem that our problems really seemed very small when one saw a brave people tirelessly digging a land out of a desert, constantly fighting off a hostile enemy.

It's a hard thing to express—the change in me. It was just that I became more aware than ever that this is a big world and that half the people in it have unbearable suffering that we Americans know little about. More, I could kind of feel it coming to a close. I knew of contemporary prophecy about Israel after working with McCall, and I knew that this brave land I had just seen was to be torn and pillaged and burned, probably in the near future. I had no idea at that time about the Yom Kippur War which was to take place a few weeks after we left. But it wouldn't have surprised me if it had started while we were there.

The only solution I could see was Christ. I resolved to dig in harder and to make my life count for more. I talked with God in great earnestness almost all the way back. I kind of "regrouped" with my Lord, putting my two-year-old Christian life in good order in my memory, wanting to make almost a new start at this point.

I had been baptized. I was completely committed. Perhaps I would never be the self-sacrificing evangelist that Lee was, or the disciplined, self-motivated soldier of Christ that Dan was, or the erudite scholar that Tom was, but I was definitely going to be all that God wanted me to be.

I faced God and told him with all of the earnestness I could muster that I was ready.

11
An Orange Carpet... and the Cadillac Suite

The first thing I was ready for was marriage.

Yvonne was one of the most difficult people to marry that I've ever encountered. When I was an unbeliever it seemed as though every girl I knew wanted to be married and tirelessly connived to that end. Some of them didn't seem to care who it might be that would someday stand up with them and say, "I do." Just so someone eventually would.

But Yvonne valued herself highly, as befits a Christian called to God's service, and she took the matter seriously. She couldn't be "talked into it." She couldn't be impressed by anything worldly.

When I returned from Israel I determined to get her to say "Yes."

I knew I desperately needed a wife. For the kind of ministry I was prayerfully headed for, I needed help. And I was in love. Men in love get married. As Ogden Nash puts it, "No matter how they tarry, eventually they marry."

Yvonne had realized by this time how strong my feelings for her were. We had both dated others during our long relationship, but always we had come back together. Any time something of significance happened to one of us, the other would be immediately informed. And for me, any time something went right in my ministry I would phone Yvonne, as if it weren't really official until she was in on it. I knew I just had to take her home someday and keep her.

She couldn't be talked into anything, I well knew, but she was a woman, and susceptible to certain propensities of her sex. While women have bizarre ways of thinking, I schemed, some things are irresistible to them.

Among these are indifference, and choosing furniture.

For the first, I simply waited for two days when I came home from Israel before calling Yvonne. That sounds easy but it wasn't. I had to grit my teeth and suffer, but I was dying to say casually, "It was a fine trip. I got back two days ago." I figured she would think, "I'm losing him!"

I got home on a Wednesday and immediately set to work finding a new apartment for Mark and me. We had moved out of our old one when I left and Mark had stayed with my family in Pittsburgh while I was away. Now we needed one immediately, and I resolved to get an unfurnished place and stop paying extra rent for furniture.

It's hard to share all the little miracles in life, but the only vacancy my favorite apartment complex had available was a large two-bedroom that Yvonne and I had once looked at together. (That was back when I stopped working for Explo, and Yvonne was along to help me pick out a new place. She had fallen in love with the orange carpet, I remembered.)

In other words, when I went to my old apartment complex the only place out of 600 they had available was that rather large apartment (suitable for a couple with one child) with that unique orange carpet Yvonne loved. She was as good as married already.

"What are you up to, Lord?" I joked as I made out the deposit check.

I should share that the name of that apartment complex is Eastgate. We know from prophecy that when the Lord returns he will enter Jerusalem, as before, through the East Gate. That kind of thing, which seems constant in my life, is somehow significant to me.

Anyway, on the following Friday I phoned Yvonne, who hadn't heard my voice for some six weeks. It was quite a conversation:

"Hello."

"Hi, Yvonne."

"Zola!"

"Yep."

"Well, for heavens sake! You're back! When did you get in?"

"Uh, let's see ... I guess it was Wednesday."

There was a long pause. "Eat your heart out," I thought to myself.

She recovered herself nicely.

"Wednesday, huh? Well, I'm very eager to see you, of course."

Making my voice elaborately casual I played my ace:

"Right. Well, if you have some time, I'd like to have you help me pick out some furniture for my new place...."

(Now you may think I was just "manuevering," playing upon my woman's weakness. Well, you're absolutely right. But I had the idea that this woman wanted to be my wife and I was within my rights to help her accomplish that.)

I picked her up after her workday, still playing it very nonchalant, while my heart was pounding in my throat at the mere sight of her. I gave her a nice kiss and told her it was great to see her again. I think I used the expression, "This is really neat," which I'd picked up at Explo. To her it meant, "It's nice to see my old buddy again." I was really laying it on.

I drove to a secondhand furniture store and turned her loose. The selection was gigantic. The place normally rented apartment furniture for modern units, but once in a while it sold off its stock. I knew Yvonne would have a ball.

Inevitably she asked me what color my carpet was.

"Orange," I said, and just left it at that. She would eventually see the apartment and realize it was the one she'd seen with me before.

Yvonne whirled through the showroom picking out a black and white decor that seemed very attractive to me. I was thinking, "Lord, let me just take her home along with the furniture. How about working something out? I'll really be good to her."

As you are probably thinking, there was a serious side to my poses. Approaching Yvonne, I'd found, was like feeding a bird. You didn't want too much fuss ... just stand there with the bread in your hand and let the birdie take it. And in this particular case I was willing to try almost anything. I was rather amazed when someone philosophized after the wedding that Yvonne was probably "on to me" all along. Love was more a woman's game, said this philosopher.

The furniture was delivered and the apartment was gorgeous. I longed to call Yvonne right away to have her come and see it, but I was still being standoffish. I knew she'd been seeing another fellow during my long absence, so I gave her the impression that she and I were growing apart.

In the meantime I kept constant touch with the Lord in Creation Central. I kept praying that Yvonne would have a real reaction of missing me.

When she saw the apartment she was duly impressed and a little moved that the Lord had brought me to this very place we'd seen earlier together. She volunteered to do a painting for the living-room wall.

I found myself phoning her every day at work, a bad old habit of mine. I would sit there at home, trying to resist calling her but dying to tell her some piece of news. I asked the Lord to act.

Finally I called her at home one Saturday night and found her very blue. The opera season was coming up, she said, and she didn't see where she would get the strength to work full-time all day and sing rehearsals every night. There was also an implication that she was very lonely.

I could almost feel the Lord tapping me on the shoulder. "Strike while the iron is hot," I thought, and I said, "I have the answer. I'm coming over right now to tell you about it."

She told me not to come, that she'd been crying and looked awful and all that. But I was a man possessed. I was determined to solve her problems and mine, right then and there.

I convinced her to let me come. When I hung up the phone I told the Lord, "This is it. I can feel it. Lord, move her tonight. Make her see it."

At Yvonne's I simply told her that I loved her very much and that she should marry me at once. Her present troubles and all future troubles would be over, and I would make her happy. I told her that I was certain this was the Lord's will.

She seemed very interested, and a bit surprised.

We agreed to pray about it, but this time for one day and no longer. I insisted on an answer the following night. I knew my customer, and myself as well. Yvonne and I were creatures of many feelings and we regularly went through changes. A delicate question like this one had to be a matter of faith, and to my knowledge, prayer is heard, recorded, and answered, instantly. If our two years of courtship hadn't shown us what we needed to know about each other, two more weeks of deliberation wouldn't help much.

While Yvonne prayed, I went around town setting up a wedding for the coming Saturday, and a honeymoon.

The next night I phoned her. Her answer was "Yes."

We spent a moment thanking the Lord together, and then I told her the wedding was in six days. She asked why it was so soon and I answered that I was now making the decisions. She was a bit taken aback, but she had the breathless sound of a girl being romanced out of her mind.

It was a busy week, as you can imagine.

McCall was out of town, but I located him by phone and asked if he could perform a wedding at the mission the following Saturday.

He said, "Sure. Who's getting married?"

I said, "Me."

He hesitated and said, "Fine. Who're you going to marry?"

McCall was one of those who had followed my campaign and thought that I had chased the girl until she caught me. He gave me heartfelt congratulations and said he would get out his book of wedding ceremonies as soon as he hit Dallas.

I arranged the blood tests with a doctor friend and the marriage license application downtown. I took Yvonne to the license office on my arm. She seemed only vaguely aware of what was happening, but I knew better.

I reserved a honeymoon room at the plush Fairmont Hotel in Dallas for the coming Saturday night and called a friend out of town for further nuptial arrangements. My friend, a doctor who had come to the Lord through correspondence with me, was living in a twenty-three-room mansion on the bend of a romantic river. He arranged to donate a wing or two to us.

I set up a place for Mark to stay during all this, and had my good suit cleaned. Then I got on the telephone and invited our guests. Then I took Yvonne to my friend the jeweler for a ring.

On the morning of my wedding day I couldn't find a clean shirt, so I ran out and bought one. Mark asked, "Are you nervous?" He was to be the best man.

Yvonne showed up at the mission, and it looked

as if the wedding was on after all. I greeted my friends who had agreed to play the piano and organ for the ceremony, and I got out the script I had written for Tom.

I had looked through the various wedding ceremonies in Tom's handbooks but none of them seemed to express the scriptural nature of marriage. So I wrote my own. I had done it the night before the wedding, along with a magazine article that had a deadline.

I stood up "at the altar" with Tom and Mark, exhausted. Only when Yvonne came down the aisle, a magnificent look of love in her eyes, did I fully realize what God had given me.

We stood shakily before Tom as he read our ceremony. We made all the right replies at the right times. Some phrases still echo in my ears:

Heavenly Father, you ordained marriage immediately at the time of creation when you said, "It is not good that man should be alone." You created a wife for Adam, the first man, and he said, "This is now bone of my bones, and flesh of my flesh.... Therefore shall a man leave his father and his mother, and shall cleave unto his wife, and they shall be one flesh...."

Zola and Yvonne, you were once strangers to each other and strangers to faith in God. You were once Jew and Gentile without God in the world. But God drew you both to him, and finally to each other. And now he has brought you to this house, together, to achieve the ultimate earthly union. You stand before us, Christian witnesses, exemplifying the holy relationship of Jesus Christ and his Church. Like that great future marriage when the Lord returns, this is a very joyous, but very solemn occasion ... Jew and Gentile, you were made one in Christ. Man and woman, you are made one in marriage....

Zola, you are a disciple of Jesus Christ, charged to love your wife as he loved the Church, to be the head of her as he was the Head of the Church, and to sacrifice for her as he sacrificed for the Church.... Yvonne, you are a disciple of Jesus Christ, charged to be subject to your husband as to the Lord, and to be holy and blameless as the bride of Christ ... Zola and Yvonne, I pronounce you husband and wife.

It all went beautifully. Especially the kiss at the end!

Afterward we went to the dining room where the mission had laid out a beautiful table. The Rev. Paul Cawthon, another missionary to the Jews, had charged out for a wedding cake just before the ceremony, and all was well.

My friend Mal Couch was the photographer. One doesn't get an internationally known film maker to take wedding stills every day.

It was a wonderful wedding, in the faithfulness of God, and with a little help from my friends.

We went downtown to the Fairmont and ran into our first hitch of this busy week. The hotel had failed to reserve our honeymoon room. The desk clerk gave me the bad news.

I stood there in shock, about to say, "You mean that after a whole week of frantic arrangements that all came off perfectly you're going to tell me I don't have a room for my wedding night!"

But the clerk saw the look in my eye. He gave me a friendly "Just a moment, sir" and disappeared into a back office. Presently he was back with good news.

"Since the error was on our part, sir, we hope you will accept a substitute room. We have no more honeymoon rooms available but we can give you the Cadillac Suite, our finest suite of rooms, at the same price. We hope you will accept, and we're really very sorry about the mix-up."

They can have my business any time. We ended up with a fantastic $120-per-day suite instead of a single room!

The McGanns' mansion was our next stop. Dr. McGann, my friend since boyhood, was extremely accommodating on this great occasion. We had the company of him and his wife and their two children as we preferred, or we had the choice, and the space, to be alone.

McGann had come to Christ after an interminable correspondence, recorded in my book *How Did a Fat, Balding, Middle-aged Jew Like You Become a Jesus Freak?* That had been McGann's first question about my faith.

A breakfast tray appeared at our door each morning for the duration of our honeymoon, and we had the advantage of observing the McGanns, a truly happy couple, at their daily living together. It was a marvelous honeymoon.

Back in Dallas, we immediately got Yvonne moved into the apartment God had chosen for us so long before. She was very comfortable with the furniture *she* had chosen for us so recently.

Life was sweet. It still is.

As a husband, as a Christian, and as a marriage counselor, I can say I have a good, good marriage!

12
How Good It Is!

If I had any lingering doubt that God was running my life our marriage has settled it.

Up to a week before the wedding I didn't know I would ever marry Yvonne, of course. And then, even having married her, I would have guessed that I was going to have a tough time adjusting to my new life.

But it's wonderful. The Bible says that the man who finds a wife finds a good thing. What an understatement. Having a loving wife, I can tell you, is better than publishing books, making films, or traveling to Israel. It's better than making money or being the center of attention.

My father used to tell a lot of Jewish jokes and one of his favorites was about a rabbi and a priest discussing their respective faiths. The priest was trying to get the rabbi to try some ham.

"Try it," he cajoled. "It's clean and it's delicious. The Jewish rules and regulations are old-fashioned. Come on, just have one sandwich!"

The rabbi said, "My friend, are you married?"

"Married?" exclaimed the priest. "Of course not!"

"Try it," said the rabbi. "It's better than ham."

Well, personally I think it's better than anything else. It's *lots* better than wrestling with sin.

Marriage seems to have the effect on me of making me serious about my work. Only recently have I fully changed from a man standing on the outside of my life, watching it sardonically, to a dedicated man. What a wife does, I think, is hold up an accurate mirror to a man, which shows what he really is. And I really want to be a worker for the Lord, before anything else. That's what my wife wants and that's what I want.

Wives aren't impressed with best-sellers, new suits, TV appearances, or film making, to my knowledge. They like the nitty-gritty. They respond to faith, hope, and love, and they regard the greatest of these to be love (1 Corinthians 13:13).

I used to think I knew a lot about women before I came to Christ. What a conceit that was! No wonder I could never seem to love them—or anybody else, for that matter.

Yvonne quit her job when we got married. We talked about this quite a bit, since my income wasn't really sufficient to cover "another mouth to feed." Even with the publisher's advances on my books and the good pay for the film venture, I was earning just enough for Mark and me.

But I thought, I'm not going to stop trusting the Lord now. He brought me a wife, in answer to my prayers. Surely he'll provide for her as he's provided for my son and myself.

I applied to the Lord for a raise and advised Yvonne to quit her job and make us a real home. It was a fine witness at the office where she worked.

People understood that one of their number was going to forego her income because she was going to be supported by God.

Don't think I'm being facetious here. Looking into my checkbook I find that my balance starting October 1973, when we returned from our honeymoon, was forty dollars.

The Lord immediately granted my raise. *The Temple*, our film made in Israel, and the book *Satan in the Sanctuary* took off like crazy. The book started to sell 10,000 copies a month and made the National Religious Paperback list. The film was shown in seventy churches on New Year's Eve.

A tour of churches was arranged for the period when the film was being shown so prolifically. Yvonne and Mark were to accompany me and take part in the programs.

So we went together as a family to serve the Lord, each doing what he could. I talked about Israel and prophecy, Yvonne sang, and Mark blew the *shofar*. The *shofar* is a ram's horn, and was the original trumpet of Leviticus 23:24. The Jews use it to call their worship together on the Feast of Trumpets, and so Mark obliged in each church at the beginning of our little program.

How Mark does this I don't know. I was a professional player of a wind instrument for many years but I can't make a sound on that archaic thing. The Bible says there are many different ministries. That one is Mark's.

I composed a song for Yvonne to sing as I played the piano. "Israel, My Love" came to me, all of a piece like my other Christian songs, during an airplane trip. I wrote it on the back of my ticket.

Music, I have noticed, is an area where the Lord does miracles for me. I had worked very hard on it as an unbeliever with no special results, like my writing. Now, as a believer, I compose much more easily, and from a technical point of view the stuff is really better than I used to turn out. My instrumental playing should have deteriorated through lack of practice, but instead it just stays or even improves. I have no fear of playing with orchestras or performing solos because, in a word, I have no fear of anything, walking with the Lord.

There's no doubt about it; when we trust our Lord and live spiritual lives, everything is better.

It may be connected with the loss of ego. I used to play music to "wow" people. Now I do it to relax or to praise the Lord. It's so much easier. I don't play for people at all; I play for the King. It's so nice to play for Someone who loves you!

The song "Israel, My Love" seemed to bring people to tears. I was a little surprised since, from my end of it, the words and music arrived in my head together and I hadn't made a single change. I taught it to Yvonne as I had received it on the airplane. Normally, musical "inspirations" have to be reworked; music is a very abstract commodity.

But this one came straight from you-know-who. I want to share it with you:

ISRAEL, MY LOVE

Refrain
    Israel, my love; Israel, my promised;
    Chosen of God, chosen for me.

Homeland forever, land of my Savior,
Israel, my love, our God watches thee.

1. Are the walls of Jerusalem standing?
   Do our fathers sleep in peace where they lay?
   Has the stranger gone? Has he left our land?
   Can we live, can we breathe, can we pray?
   Does the Jew stand fast in Galilee?
   Does the Jordan still flow from the sea?
   Can the Lord come home to the land he loved?
   Can we live, can we pray, can we be?
           (Repeat Refrain)

2. Does the rose still bloom in the desert?
   Does the olive tree bask in the sun?
   Do the children laugh, are the soldiers home?
   Is the age-old fighting done?
   Has Messiah come, has the King returned?
   Are we saved? Oh, blest be he!
   When the King comes home to the land he loves
   We can live, we can pray, we can be.*
           (Repeat Refrain)

You don't find many Hebrew Christian songs.
Hopefully, when "Israel, My Love" is distributed it
will testify about the special place of Israel in the
hearts of Christians, Jews, and unbelievers alike.
"Pray for the peace of Jerusalem."

That brings us pretty much up to date. I can't
share too far ahead. I don't know if God will still
want me writing or film making. Maybe he'll want
me to be a musician or a marriage counselor again.
Maybe he'll want me in some other field I've never

---

*From *Israel, My Love,* by Zola Levitt, © 1975 Moody
Press, Moody Bible Institute of Chicago. Used by permission.

imagined before. Maybe he'll want me broke and struggling again. Maybe he'll call me home to him.

I have no preferences. His will be done.

Epilogue

The apostles got a lot of mileage out of letters, so I'm going to write three letters below to my three groups of friends: Christians, Jews, and unbelievers.

God has grouped you, not I. He regards the Christian, the Jew, and the unbeliever differently in the Scriptures, though all people become "one in Christ" when they are saved.

There are different things I want to say to the different groups. These are the views of a very young Christian for what they're worth.

Dear friends in Christ,

I don't understand Christians very well, in the manner that children don't understand adults very well. But we all have noticed that children once in a while shed light on things for us. The Bible says, "Out of the mouths of babes ...."

I want to say that joy and happiness in life are not sinful. This seems too obvious to say, but I've seen many people trying to live lives of rules and regulations until they're so messed up they're of little use to the Lord or to their neighbors.

I get the feeling that men make up rules and regulations because they have little faith. They think God won't perfect them if they don't take steps of their own. They leave little for God to do when they lock up their personalities in grand gestures of religiosity. I say, let's check our behavior against Scripture, not against "local opinion."

Another thing I want to say is this: every Christian should be up-to-date on prophecy.

Today we are watching prophecy being fulfilled. We are the generation who saw Israel regathered to her land. We are likely to be the generation to see the Russian invasion of Israel prophesied by Ezekiel.

Christianity has become God's "evacuation plan" for the earth. Christ, and only Christ, will get us out of the mess we've made in the world. If the unbeliever is made to realize that, you won't have to sing him any hymns to get him to Christ.

And I want to say this too—take some chances on God. "Ye have not because ye ask not," says the Scripture, and I think we ask not because we don't really think we're going to receive anything. Despite God's demonstrations of love toward us I get the feeling that we don't really think he's going to come through.

Well, I've taken wild chances on God and he's come through loud and clear. I'm not telling you to quit your job and look for support from heaven —unless that's what God moves you to do. But I am saying that he's a better, more faithful God than many people give him credit for.

Ask him for what you want. You'll be amazed.

And converse with him. Our Jesus is represented as a God who cared about flowers and sparrows. He had time for everybody. When the Samaritan woman tried to involve him in theological tangles about worship, he set her straight in plain words. Worship in spirit and in truth, was what he said, not in archaic dialects or forced sanctimony. Talk to him all day, in your own words. I've found him to be a terrific listener.

And last, care for Israel. This isn't just a personal request. Israel is God's home on the earth. It was and it will be.

God promised Abraham that he would bless those who blessed his descendants, the Jews. And so he has. America, a place where the Jew has been able to live without fear and persecution, has prospered tremendously. Remember the Jews in your prayers. In a sense they gave us all we have. Jesus, and all his disciples and apostles were Jews. All those first Christians, who bravely worshiped the Son of God in Jerusalem back at the beginning, were Jews. The men who wrote our blessed Bible were Jews.

I am a Levite, consecrated by God to bless his people in his name (Deuteronomy 10:8) and so I do. God bless you, every one.

> *In his love,*
> *zl*

141

Dear Jewish brothers,

These are tough times for us, but when have we had it easy? Tevye said to God, "I know we're your chosen people. But why don't you choose somebody else for a while?"

We know just what he meant by that.

If the world realized how we fought and ran and died to have our plain little land, there would be no Yom Kippur wars. But they never have understood and they never will. Sympathy we'll never get.

Brothers, I want to say something that's obnoxious to you, but it's a deep conviction of mine.

This conviction is that Jesus was our Messiah. And he is our Messiah. He will deliver us from our troubles just as our Messiah is supposed to do. I have experienced this, as you have seen.

Please understand, we have our God and he hears us. But he made a bargain with us—a new covenant—in Jeremiah 31:31-34, and we haven't held up our end of the bargain. Our Scriptures promised us a Messiah, remission of our sins, and ultimate salvation to God. But a portion of our ancestors failed to recognize Jesus for who he was, and the rest of us have followed suit. As with those kosher laws, we have blindly followed the past.

Now with us, of course, it's a different thing. We don't follow tradition because we're stupid; we follow it because we have to have something to hold on to. No other people has had anything like our experience of 2,000 years of hounding and persecution. What do they know of traditions anyway? We've fooled them, our persecutors. Their civilizations disappear, like the Babylonians, but ours goes on and on, gloriously in our traditions.

But those are dealings with men. Dealings with God are another matter. Our Scriptures tell us that our ancestors had hard times because they weren't faithful to God, and the lesson still applies.

I want to refer you to my book, Jesus—the Jews' Jew. The last chapter was written exclusively for you, my brothers. It's called "For Jews Only." And it shows, from our Testament, which the goyim call the "Old" Testament, that Jesus was our proper Messiah. You don't need the so-called "New" Testament to come to the Messiah.

Now I like the New Testament, personally. I'm partial to Jewish writing to begin with. But I offer to you only our own Scriptures because I know you trust them.

You I don't have to tell how to pray. But I want to suggest a certain kind of prayer. Say to God, "If Jesus is my Messiah, I want him in my life."

And watch what happens!

L'chaim
ZELIG FIVEL
BEN YOSEF
LEIB HALEVI

Dear unbelieving friend,

I love you. I would be a rotten Christian if I didn't. But I do for still better reasons. I followed your way of doing things for most of my life and I know just where you're at.

You know me well enough to know I'm no fanatic. Sometimes I think some Christians are plain nuts, and I can understand why you keep your distance.

But know this, Jesus doesn't require you to go nuts to follow him. There are dynamic people leading rational, effective lives who believe in Christ, and they're going to change the world, I can tell you.

In the manner that I've found a new way of life, anybody can. I wasn't any sort of fanatic about spiritual things when I came to Jesus; he's taken care of any changes that were necessary, with little effort from me. If a Christian tells you you have to change yourself inside out to come to Christ, don't believe him. The thief on the cross was perfectly acceptable to our Lord even though he was right then being executed. All he did was express a little faith.

Bible prophecy is a matter you should know something about. Does it surprise you that the Bible long ago forecasted an alliance between Russia and Arab powers to invade Israel? Or for that matter, did you know the Bible, and only the Bible, announced that Israel would someday be resettled by Jews who would come out of foreign countries?

I say "only the Bible" because who else, in his right mind, would ever really have thought the

Jews would reoccupy their homeland after nineteen centuries?

To me, life without a spiritual grasp of things is insipid floundering, based on the latest pop philosophy and incessant searching for ways out of depression. That's what I felt, and I think that about says it.

Save yourself a lot of trouble and get with it. Remember, all I ever said to Jesus was, "If you're there, show me." If you believe what I've written down in this book, you've seen what happened.

I've sat with depressed people in clinics and I've seen that they haven't any idea which way to turn. They can be comforted and helped by sound psychological advice, if they're not too far gone. But inevitably, the thing that helps them is love, from outside themselves. That's just the nature of the machine.

Well, I find that love from Above is more curative, more speedy, and infinitely more complete.

Close this book and say, "If you're there, show me," or whatever you want to say along those lines.

And I guarantee you, we'll meet again!

To you, in Christ,
zl